Literature-Based
Seasonal and Holiday Activities

MARY BETH SPANN

SCHOLASTIC
PROFESSIONAL BOOKS

New York • Toronto • London • Auckland • Sydney

**With love,
to my sweet daughter, Francesca,
who celebrates each of her days with wonder,
and fills all of mine with joy.**

Acknowledgments

I wish to extend my deepest gratitude to Harriette Vedder, Sea Cliff
Elementary School Librarian, North Shore School District, Sea Cliff, New
York, for her work in compiling long lists of quality seasonal and holiday
books to use with children, *and* for allowing me to borrow a carload of
the school's library books for this project. (Everyone should have a friend
like Harriette.) Also, endless thanks to my dear friends and colleagues
Connie Turner, Russ Clinton, and Debby Dixler, who generously offered their
expert advice and ideas, and to the Shoreham-Wading River New York Public
Librarian, Lori Blend, who actually let me sneak home with a copy of *Books
in Print.* Hugs to my husband and his family who were always there to help
out with loving offers of child care. And, a final tip of the hat to Scholastic
editor, Terry Cooper, for her intelligent insights, honest critiques, patience,
direction, and enthusiasm . . . and for giving me a chance in the first place.

Designed by Nancy Metcalf
Production by Intergraphics
Cover design by Vincent Ceci
Cover illustration by Beth Glick
Illustrations by Anna Cota-Robles

ISBN 0-590-49134-2

Printed in the U.S.A.

CONTENTS

continued

Spring Celebrations 79

INTRODUCTION

For decades, seasonal and holiday celebrations have made the school year go 'round. But, the classroom celebrations of today are more than confetti and cupcakes. They are ways to get students in touch with traditions and history. They help mark passages, elevate awareness of the many traditions and practices represented in the multicultural classroom, and offer opportunities to educate in a meaningful context.

One great way to introduce a unit on a holiday or seasonal celebration is to share a relevant piece of literature with your class. But hunting down the perfect book for an occasion takes precious planning time—so we did the work for you!

Literature-Based Seasonal and Holiday Activities serves up a selection of best-loved book titles designed to help you introduce and share 25 holiday and seasonal celebrations with your class. A brief book summary will acquaint you with the story line of each title. To help you focus on the themes presented in each book, we provide theme-related introductory explorations: probing questions, reflections, and preliminary activities guaranteed to pique interest while building on prior knowledge. A section of book-based follow-up activities helps you use the literature to expand childrens' concrete experience. For your students' learning pleasure, we've also included one enrichment reproducible activity page designed to accompany each book.

After each book selection, we have recommended grade levels, but feel free to experiment. Sometimes a chapter book is perfect to share (in small bites) with young children, just as a wordless picture book can be used effectively with older children. Remember, you know your students best.

While this book focuses on traditional American celebrations, we have selected books with characters and settings reflecting a variety of ages, races, and cultures. By sharing books that represent a spectrum of peoples and situations, students will do more than celebrate red-letter days and dates. With this literature-based approach, they will also begin to appreciate and embrace every day as a special season or holiday of the heart!

Fall Celebrations

Mousekin's Golden House

by Edna Miller
(Simon & Schuster, 1964)

Mousekin's curiosity is tickled when he comes upon a discarded Halloween jack-o'-lantern. Danger forces Mousekin inside the pumpkin, where he discovers a "beautiful golden room—just the right size for a little mouse." As autumn turns to winter, Mousekin finds the security he needs in the safety of the golden pumpkin house.

Exploring Themes of Taking Chances and Feeling Safe

❍ Mousekin is very curious about the Halloween jack-o'-lantern. Invite the children to tell what they know about curiosity. Do they know any other stories about curious characters? Have them tell about times when they were curious. How do they behave when they are curious? If they were in Mousekin's place, would they have jumped inside the pumpkin? Why or why not?

❍ Once inside the pumpkin, Mousekin fills his new house with things to keep him cozy and warm. Have the children remember what Mousekin does to feel comfortable, and then talk about things we do to "cozy-up" our rooms at home and in school.

| FOLLOW-UP ACTIVITIES |

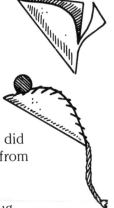

Curious Mouse Bookmarks

For each mouse bookmark, you will need: one piece of tan felt (3-inch square), one 9-inch long piece of brown rug yarn, a large paper clip, markers, yarn needles, embroidery floss, glue, and scissors. Fold felt square in half, creating triangle. Use scissors to trim top corner of triangle as indicated. Open felt square and place end of yarn on fold inside square. Glue yarn "tail" in place and spread more glue to edge of felt. Press closed. Cut small circles from scrap felt and glue circles on mouse to indicate ears. At raw edge of felt, use marker to make dots indicating where needle and thread should go. Help students sew overhand stitches to finish raw edges of bookmarks.

Cozy Collectibles

Host a cozy-time "bring 'n brag" session. Have children remember what Mousekin did to make his golden house warm and cozy. Then invite children to bring one item from home that makes them feel especially snug and secure. Items could range from a favorite milk mug to a cuddly teddy bear. After children share their items with the group, use tables and bulletin boards to create a cozy display labeled "Feeling Snug as a Mouse in a Golden House."

Pumpkin Sequence Story Booklets

Carve a jack-o'-lantern face into a pumpkin. Also cut shapes from scraps of the pumpkin to use as stamps. For each child, cut two large pumpkin shapes from orange construction paper. Have children print faces onto one paper pumpkin by dipping the pumpkin pieces into black tempera paint and then pressing onto the paper. Then give each child a copy of page 9. Have children discuss the pictures. Each child can then color the pictures (if desired), cut them apart, and arrange them on the second paper pumpkin in sequence. Glue in place. Let dry and staple jack-o'-lantern face pumpkin on top of story sequence pumpkin, creating a story booklet.

Mousekin's Golden House

Sequence Pictures Recapping Story

1

2

3

4

The Ghost-Eye Tree

by Bill Martin, Jr. and John Archambault
(Henry Holt, 1985)

Dark and eerie images of an autumn night surround two children sent on an errand to the end of town. Imaginations run rampant and fears mount as the children anticipate coming upon the haunting ghost-eye tree.

Exploring Themes of Fear and Bravery

○ Are some seasons and some times scarier than others? Why did the authors choose an autumn night as the setting for this story? Tell why the story would or would not work as well if it took place on a spring night or a summer day?

○ The children in the book are afraid to pass the ghost-eye tree, but they try to be brave. Sometimes they deny their fears, or they sing to lift their spirits. And the boy wears a hat to make himself feel tough. Have the children share times they have been afraid. List each on a large chart pad. Challenge students to write down solutions to each situation. Compare and contrast results. How many different solutions did the group come up with?

FOLLOW-UP ACTIVITIES

Reader's Theatre

The Ghost-Eye Tree was written to be read aloud as a reader's theatre piece. Divide your class into groups and have the children take turns reading portions of the book aloud. After several practice sessions, record your reading and have the children listen to the tape. What do they notice about the rhythm and rhymes of the book's language? Are there places where their reading automatically quickened? Which parts sounded the spookiest?

Autumn Night Art

After studying the tree illustrations in the *Ghost-Eye Tree*, have children create their own renditions of a scary autumn night. Provide them with crayons and large pieces of yellow construction paper and instruct them to draw an outdoor autumn night scene. Dilute black tempera paint with water and brush "wash" over completed drawings.

Autumn Imagery

As a springboard for this activity, have the children reread *The Ghost-Eye Tree* noting any descriptive imagery (feelings, moods, etc.) the text and illustrations present. Distribute copies of page 11. With the word *tree* as your first noun, have students first generate a list of other autumn nouns (*school, apples, cider, leaves, pumpkins, Thanksgiving, football, harvest,* etc.). Then have them come up with a list of adjectives describing each noun.

Have children use these lists to write about a typical autumn day or night in their neighborhood. Remind children to include as much description as possible so that the readers will really see and feel the images in the essays.

The Ghost-Eye Tree

Nouns	tree	apple			
Adjectives		red crisp			
Nouns					
Adjectives					

Timothy Goes to School

by Rosemary Wells
(Dial Press, 1981)

Timothy sets off for the first day of school with high hopes, only to return home at the end of the day in tears. Timothy's struggles to fit in at his new school are tenderly recounted in this book about fitting in and friendship.

Exploring Themes of Fitting in and Feeling Loved

❍ Timothy is very excited about going to school, but after the first day, he returns home feeling very sad. Talk with the children about how they felt on their first day of school. Did any of them have more than one feeling at a time (excited and scared)? Talk about the physical manifestations of each feeling. (Look at the illustrated body language in the book. Have children note and compare how Timothy is depicted as he sets off for school versus how he appears as he returns home.)

❍ In school, Timothy meets Claude and tries to be his friend. But Claude keeps making fun of Timothy's school clothes, and Timothy finds himself wishing bad things would happen to Claude. Ask the children to talk (without naming names!) about times they've tried unsuccessfully to make friends. How did they feel? (Remind children that all feelings are okay to have, but we may not always act on our negative feelings—especially if our actions will hurt someone.)

FOLLOW-UP ACTIVITIES

Secret Pal Snack Swap

When Timothy comes home from school, his mother always has a snack waiting for him. At the end of the story, Timothy invites Violet to come home with him for some cookies. Invite your class to show they care for each other by hosting a snack swap. Provide large, round crackers, and an assortment of toppings (peanut butter, cream cheese, raisins, apple slices, shredded carrots, shredded cheese, sliced grapes, banana "coins," slivered almonds, cereal circles, etc.). On a blackboard or bulletin board, create a large grid. Print each of the children's names on the left hand side of the grid, and the individual names of the snack ingredients on the bottom of the grid. Meet with the children and have them indicate on the grid which foods they would like included on their snack crackers. (Be aware of and sensitive to any special dietary restrictions.) Have children draw names of classmates from a hat. Each child then refers to the grid and prepares a snack for his or her "secret pal." Snacks may be left at each child's place with a signed note from the creator.

Raccoon Paper Doll

Part of Timothy's problem stems from the outfits he wears to school. Give each child a copy of page 13 and invite children to design clothing a raccoon would like to wear. When completed, glue each page on construction paper and laminate (or cover with clear adhesive) for durability. Cut out raccoon dolls and cloths and place together in a community paper-doll box for some free-play fun.

Anabelle Swift, Kindergartner

by Amy Schwartz
(Orchard Books, 1988)

Big sister Lucy offers Anabelle some unorthodox advice to prepare her for her first day at kindergarten. The advice steers Anabelle in the wrong direction. But, by relying on her own abilities and confidence, Annabelle manages to turn her first day of school into a rousing success!

Exploring the Theme of Self-Reliance

❍ Lucy gives some advice to her sister. Why does Lucy tell Anabelle how to behave in school? Ask the children how it feels to give help and advice. Have they ever helped anyone out? Do people ever give them advice? How do they know whether the advice will work out or not? Are some people better advice-givers than others? Make a list of reliable advice-givers both at home and in school.

❍ Ask the children if the book *Anabelle Swift, Kindergartner* could be a true story? Why or why not? Do they know any real people like Lucy or Anabelle? Did anything in the story every happen to them? Have children write about their first day of kindergarten. How did they look? What did the classroom look like? Have them include descriptions of the other kids and the teacher. Did anything funny happen? Encourage children to interview family members about their first days at school.

FOLLOW-UP ACTIVITIES

Silly Idioms

When Anabelle feels embarassed in school she wants to "crawl under the rug." Ask children what the author meant by this. (Did Anabelle *really* want to crawl under the rug?) Offer the children a list of popular idioms such as: "Go jump in the lake." "He drove me up the wall," and "I'm keeping an eye on you." Discuss the figurative meaning of each. Invite children to print their favorites on pieces of drawing paper, literally interpret them, and then illustrate them. Display the labeled illustrations on a bulletin board entitled, "Having a Whale of a Time With Idioms!"

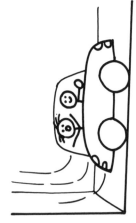

You're driving me up the wall.

Money-Exchange Game

Anabelle's great talent is her ability to count numbers past 100. Here's a money-counting game that will have small groups of students counting and regrouping numbers as represented by real coins. First, provide each player with a copy of the game board on page 15. Also provide players with a pair of dice and a dish full of change—approximately 100 pennies, 100 dimes, and a dollar bill. (If you wish, plastic chips or play money may be used.) To play, children roll dice and count out the correct number of pennies as determined by the number on the dice. They then place the coins on the corresponding gameboard spots. When the row of pennies is full, players may exchange pennies for a dime. The same procedure is used to exchange dimes for a dollar. The first child to exchange coins up to one dollar wins.

1    6    1    6

2    7    2    7

3    8   3    8

4    9    4    9

5    10    5    10

Pennies   ## Dimes

Dollar

The Wall

by Eve Bunting
(Clarion Books, 1990)

The Vietnam Veterans Memorial in Washington, D.C., is the focal point of this moving book about war and remembering. As we watch a boy and his father on their visit to the wall, we see how war continues to affect generations with a legacy of pain and loss.

Exploring Themes of War, Honor, and Loss

○ Ask the children to talk about how they felt after reading *The Wall*. Since "nothing bad" happens in the book, ask the children how the author's story could leave us feeling so sad or unhappy. Ask children if we should or should not read books that do not have a happy ending.

○ War memorials are erected to honor people who fought and died for a cause. The structures also remind us of the pain war brings. These reminders encourage us to work toward peaceful solutions in the future. In the book, the teacher visiting the wall says, "The names are of the dead. But the wall is for all of us." Ask the class what they think the teacher meant. Show the children pictures of other war memorials and ask them why they think we build and visit such sites. Encourage as many answers as possible. List the reasons the children come up with on the chalkboard or on a chart pad. Guide them to explore possible political and personal reasons for erecting such permanent reminders of war.

FOLLOW-UP ACTIVITIES

Memory Boxes

The people visiting the wall left trinkets and reminders for their loved ones who died. In doing so, the living can remain connected to deceased family members and friends. Share with the group some object that holds special meaning or memories for you. Impress students with the concept that such "treasures" need not be expensive or important to others. Have children bring and share one trinket or remembrance that is most special to them. Then have children create memory storage boxes. For each box you will need a shoe box, cloth tape, paint, scissors, and markers or stickers. Paint the shoe boxes. Let dry. Create a hinged lid on the shoe box by first taping the lid to the box along one long edge, and then slitting the lid at the two corners that are taped to the box. Decorate boxes with markers or stickers. Students can use finished boxes to store memorabilia.

Visitors to the Wall

Reread *The Wall* and this time notice all the different people who come to visit the memorial. Provide students with copies of page 17. Tell the class that each of the visitors may have different reasons for visiting the wall. Have children speculate on why each of the visitors in the book (including the boy and his father, the soldier in a wheelchair, the old woman and old man, the school girls, the teacher, the grandfather and the grandson) came to the wall. Have children note how the visitors may be feeling as they visit the wall. Instruct children to record their ideas on the sheet. Share the recorded thoughts with the class.

The Wall

Who Visited *The Wall* and Why?

Visitors	Reasons

The Butter Battle Book

by Dr. Seuss
(Random House, 1984)

Told from the viewpoint of a child, The Butter Battle Book *is the story of two neighboring communities at war because they cannot agree on the correct way to butter bread. The two groups each develop bigger and better weapons to fight their war, but the initial problem remains unsolved. The book's conclusion leaves the reader wondering which side will drop a bomb that will end the dispute—and both civilizations.*

Exploring Themes of Disagreement and Resolutions

❍ The characters in *The Butter Battle Book* begin their war with a disagreement. Ask: How does it feel when we are in agreement with someone else? How does it feel when we disagree? Why would disagreement make some people (like the characters in the book) feel like fighting?

❍ Have students explain why some people believe that fighting is the best way to solve a problem. Ask students to offer their own opinions about fighting. (This is just an information gathering session—resist the urge to modify students' opinions.) Ask the students to support their beliefs with examples from their own experiences with disagreements and fighting.

FOLLOW-UP ACTIVITIES

Peace Machines

Offer students shoe boxes and recycled or leftover art supplies (empty cardboard tubes, oaktag, plastic foam packing material, pipe cleaners, foil, wooden shapes, paints, markers, tape, glue, etc.). Challenge students to work in groups to design peace machines. Then have children write essays describing the peace-making features of their machines.

Peaceful Story Conclusion

Invite students to extend the story presented in *The Butter Battle Book*. Does either Grandpa or Van Itch decide to drop the bomb? Could the boy in the book change what seems to be a sealed fate? You might want to have some students write a positive conclusion while others write a disastrous conclusion.

Conflict-Resolution Cards

Copy page 19 and cut apart the cards. Place them in a box and have students take turns selecting cards at random. After reading each card to the class, divide students into small groups and have them work together to discuss and list a variety of nonviolent ways to solve each problem. Combine the lists to create one large list. Refer to list when real-life conflicts arise.

The Butter Battle Book

Conflict Resolution Cards

One of the kids in your class won't stop teasing you. What should you do?

A bully wants to fight you after school (says you're chicken if you don't fight). What should you do?

You have a best friend, but he or she wants to play with someone else. What should you do?

You were looking forward to eating the cookies in the cookie jar at home after school, but you find out your brother ate them all and didn't leave you any! What should you do?

Every time you try to get a turn on the playground equipment, a bigger kid pushes you off. What should you do?

You saw someone take your friend's crayons but are afraid of getting in trouble if you tell. What should you do?

Sequoya

by Jan Gleiter and Kathleen Thompson
(Raintree Children's Books, 1988)

This biography recounts the life of Sequoya, a Cherokee Indian who invented a system of writing. Readers are helped to understand how Sequoya's efforts "did more for his people than if he had given each one a bag of gold."

Exploring Themes of Curiosity and Determination

○ Ask the group to tell what it means to be curious. Have any of the children in the class ever felt curious? What do they do when they feel curious? Ask them to give examples of Sequoya's curiosity. What did Sequoya's do when he felt curious?

○ Have children imagine all the feelings Sequoya may have felt when his work was destroyed by fire. After the fire, wouldn't it have been easier for Sequoya to give up and quit his work? What lesson can we learn from Sequoya's example? Have the children talk about times they felt like giving up, but didn't.

FOLLOW-UP ACTIVITIES

Stylish Letters

Help students develop an appreciation for the power of alphabet design. Begin by having children collect cardboard packaging from food, soap, toys, advertisements, etc. Display these (collage style) on a bulletin board. Have the children identify, contrast, and compare the assorted attributes of the type styles collected (bold and blocky, thin and curly, etc.). Help children discover that different kinds of print are used for different purposes and to evoke different moods or feelings (for example, print used to advertise a baby doll may look different from print used to advertise toy trucks). Have children design stylish name tags for their desks. Have them choose a favorite print style from the display, then, using pencils and colorful markers, write their names on strips of oaktag in that style.

Multicultural Alphabets

Send your class on an alphabet hunt to discover communication systems other than our 26-letter alphabet. Many cultures and languages feature their own alphabet system. Have children begin their search in the pages of the encyclopedia. Librarians will be able to support your search with additional books and resource materials. Plan visits to museums with a special eye on alphabet-related materials.

Class Newspaper

One of the greatest gifts Sequoya offered his people was the ability to create a newspaper. With this in mind, use copies of page 21 to publish your own class newspaper. Have students work individually, in pairs, or in small groups to report, write, and produce the news. Make enough copies of each edition for each student to own a copy. Bind one copy of each edition in a looseleaf notebook labeled "Noteworthy Classroom News."

NEWSPAPER

_____

This week's reporters: Date _____

Here's What We're Learning About . . .

Books We've Been Reading

Personality Profile of the Week

Upcoming Events

The Legend of the Indian Paintbrush

retold by Tomie dePaola
(G. P. Putnam's Sons, 1988)

Here's the legend of how the brilliant and beautiful Indian paintbrush plant received its name. As the boy known as Little Gopher fulfills his Dream-Vision, we can feel and appreciate our own connection to the spirit of nature.

Exploring Themes of Dreams and Sacrifice

○ How is the Dream-Vision that came to Little Gopher the same and how is it different from the dreams we dream when we are asleep? How is the Dream-Vision the same and how is it different from the wishing kind of dreams? Fold a large piece of drawing paper in half. On one side draw a sleep-dream and on the other draw a wish-dream. Describe these dreams to the class.

○ Little Gopher sometimes "longed to put aside his brushes and ride out with the warriors. But, he always remembered his Dream-Vision and he did not go with them." Why did Little Gopher's Dream-Vision keep him from going with the warriors? Couldn't he just paint sometimes? Have you ever had to make sacrifices for something you really wanted? How does it feel to make such choices? How does it feel when a goal (or a vision) is realized?

FOLLOW-UP ACTIVITIES

Still Lifes

Have children research the bluebonnet and the Indian paintbrush. Read *The Legend of the Bluebonnet* by Tomie dePaola. Locate both plants in the encyclopedia. Look on a map to find Texas and Wyoming—homes of the Indian paintbrush and the bluebonnet. If possible, show the children real or artificial samples of the two plants. Arrange them in a vase and have the children paint still lifes.

Creating "Animal Canvases"

In the book, Little Gopher collects animal skins. He stretches and pulls these skins tight on wooden frames. On these skins, he uses symbols to paint pictures of great hunts, deeds, and dreams. Simulate the look of painted animal skins. For each "canvas" you will need a plain brown grocery bag, paints, and scissors. Trim away the bottom of the bag. Cut down the sides of the bag to create two canvases. Roughly trim each canvas to resemble an animal skin. Crumple the bag into a ball. Smooth open and crumple again. Repeat until the wrinkled paper has the look and feel of leather. Paint symbols, sunsets, or dreams on the canvases. Hang completed canvases from sticks or dowels made from lengths of rolled oaktag. Add yarn fringe if desired.

Use page 23 for Native American symbol ideas to paint on your canvases.

The Legend of the Indian Paintbrush

Native American Symbols

friendly camp   lake   hear   night

canoe   camp   fish   mountain

bravest   blanket   see   stars

talk together   lightning   little brave   rain

Christopher Columbus: A Great Explorer

by Carol Greene
(Children's Press, 1989)

Here unfolds the fascinating (and sometimes unsettling) life of Christopher Columbus. The text is richly embroidered with historic paintings, sketches, and diagrams documenting the life and times of Columbus. The reader is treated to a vivid picture of how scary and exhilarating it must have been to set sail with Columbus on his quest for discoveries and wealth.

Exploring Themes of Dreams and Risk-Taking

○ Columbus was a dreamer who made his dreams come true. Ask the class to cite examples of how Columbus made his dreams into reality. Ask: How would the story of Christopher Columbus be different if he had just hoped for his dream to come true?

○ Columbus took many chances in his life. Ask the class to talk about opportunities they've had to take chances. How does it feel to take risks? Does each risk-taking experience feel the same? Is it always good to take risks? Discuss the positive and negative aspects of being a risk-taker.

FOLLOW-UP ACTIVITIES

Perilous Paintings

Examine the variety of illustrations of Columbus's dangerous voyages. Then provide paints and paper and have students paint their own renditions of the scenes. Have children first sketch their ideas on paper and then with paints. (Encourage them to create large-scale sketches which are a bit easier to paint.) Set aside time for children to describe their paintings to the group. During this exercise, stress the importance of a variety of artistic interpretations. Display paintings on a bulletin board labeled, "The Voyages of Christopher Columbus."

Voyage Log

Have children pretend they sailed with Columbus. Invite them to create log entries recounting their voyage. Have students research and recount the facts so that their fictional logs may be based in reality.

Risk-Taking Adventures

Help students understand that the better informed they are regarding risk-taking opportunities, the better choices they will make. To begin, make several copies of page 25, which features descriptions of open-ended situations. Cut strips apart, fold, and place in a shoe box. Working with a small group of students, ask one student from the group to step into the hallway while another draws one strip from the box and reads it aloud. Then, have the group brainstorm the pros and cons of taking the risk described. Record ideas on the blackboard or on a piece of chart paper. When the other student rejoins the group, read the strip again and have the student spontaneously choose whether or not to take the risk. The group then shares their list of pros and cons, and the student has a chance to reconsider. Play continues until all students in the group have had a chance to participate.

Christopher Columbus

A strange dog approaches you on the school yard. You like dogs and want to pet this one. What do you do?

At school, the writing club is holding a contest. You think you have some good entry ideas, but you're afraid the judges won't like them. What do you do?

There's a new kid in class. The rest of the class doesn't like her. You feel sorry for the new kid and want to make friends. What do you do?

You go skiing with some friends. They want to take you on a very high slope. You're terrified. What do you do?

All of your friends have signed up to take swimming lessons. You want to sign up, too, but you're a terrible swimmer and would feel awful if your friends saw you swim. What do you do?

The people who live next door to you just had a new baby. You'd love to offer to babysit, but don't know how to tell them without feeling silly. What do you do?

Your teacher wants everyone to give an oral book report. You hate speaking in front of the class and are thinking about staying home that day. What do you do?

Watch the Stars Come Out

by Riki Levinson
(E. P. Dutton, 1985)

This book recounts the bittersweet journey of a little red-haired girl and her brother, who must travel alone to join their parents in America. The travelers' one bright star is the Statue of Liberty—a glittering beacon in a strange new world.

Exploring Themes of Starting Over and Storytelling

○ Discuss the definition of immigration. How many of the children have ancestors who were (or are) immigrants? Are any of the children in the group immigrants? Locate the countries of origin on a map. The families portrayed in this book left their homes for new homes in a new country. Ask the children to find out from older family members and friends why so many people risked such a difficult journey to start over.

○ The structure of the book is that of a story within a story. After having the students research their families' roots (as suggested above), ask each student to tell his or her own family's story about coming to live where they do. If possible, have parents or grandparents visit the class to tell their stories and to answer questions (prepared ahead of time) about immigration and countries of origin.

FOLLOW-UP ACTIVITIES

Stories in the Stars

Provide students with black construction paper, foil stars, and white chalk. After reviewing pictures of constellations with students, have them create their own "stories in the stars." Have students use chalk to draw or trace shapes (animals, vehicles, etc.) on the paper and then glue stars to several points on the pictures. Students may write essays describing the myths behind their constellations.

Pack Your Bags

Have students pretend they are going on a long, one-way journey to a new country. They may only take one suitcase. Provide each student with a file folder meant to represent a suitcase. Use markers to decorate the outside of the folders to resemble suitcases. On the inside of the suitcases, have the children list and then draw what they would take on their journey. "Lock" the suitcases with paper clips and glue on a c-shaped handle cut from brown construction paper. Have children describe the contents of their suitcases and the rationale for their choices.

Multicultural Lady Liberty Statue Collage

Using an overhead projector, enlarge the pattern on page 27 until the projected image is approximately 3 feet tall. Trace the pattern onto butcher paper and cut it out. Provide students with a supply of magazines. Help them cut out a variety of faces from the magazines. Have children sort the pictures by size (small, medium, and large) and begin gluing the large faces on the statue, leaving space between pictures. Fill in spaces with medium-sized pictures and then small pictures, overlapping edges as you glue. As a finishing touch, add pictures of the students to the collage and glue in place. Tape the multicultural statue to a doorway or a wall to greet visitors to your school. (As a variation, each student may make smaller, individual versions of this project.)

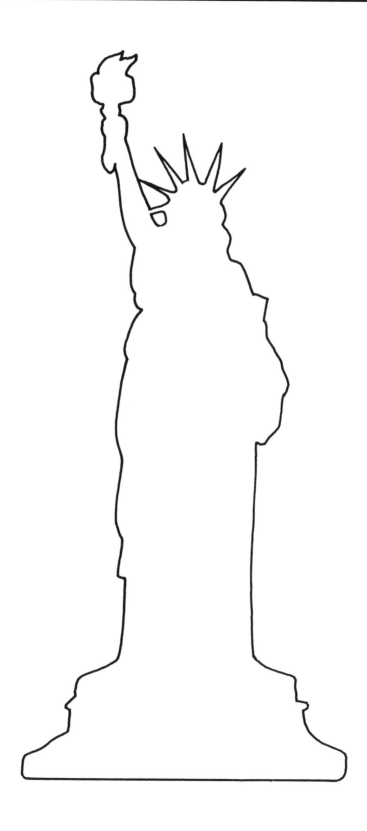

The Story of the Statue of Liberty

by Betsy and Giulio Maestro
(Lothrop, Lee & Shepard Books, 1986)

This book showcases the construction of the Statue of Liberty. The drama of the statue's creation is heightened by a look at the statue's own journey to the new world where Lady Liberty was finally erected as an eternal symbol of liberty and refuge.

Exploring Themes of Cooperation and Dreams Come True

❍ The people who designed and constructed the Statue of Liberty worked together until she was complete. Have the children recall times they worked together towards a common goal. Why can it be easier to finish a job when you have help? When is it easier to work alone?

❍ It took 21 years for the dream of the Statue of Liberty to come true. Help the children understand the difference between long-term and short-term goals and dreams. On a piece of chart paper (or on the blackboard) make a list of short-term and long-term dreams. Ask the children why it's important to have both in our lives.

> FOLLOW-UP ACTIVITIES

Lady Liberty Fireworks Pop-up Paintings

Pour colorful paints into dishes. Add a few drops of glue. Place dollops of paint on construction paper. Have children use their fingers to spread the paint out from center. Sprinkle with glitter. When dry, cut out fireworks explosion and attach them to a piece of black construction paper with small strips of stiff paper folded accordion style. If desired, cut out and glue on paper silhouette details such as water, boats, and the statue.

Liberty Big Book

Have the class work together to create a Big Book that retells the story of the Statue of Liberty. First, have children dictate the story of the Statue of Liberty in their own words. Guide the session to make certain the facts and sequence of events are accurate. Record their story on a large chart pad. Divide the class into pairs and assign each pair one or two sentences of the story. Give each group a large sheet of scrap paper and direct them to write their assigned lines at the bottom of the page. Have students decide what their accompanying illustrations will be and draw them. Ask for student volunteers to make a cover and a title page for the book. Punch holes in the pages and bind them together with loose-leaf rings.

Lady Liberty's Point of View

Give each child a copy of page 29 on which to retell and record the story of the Statue of Liberty from Lady Liberty's point of view. Have children imagine that they are being put together (and taken apart again) for the long voyage to America. How does it feel to be a famous statue people visit? How does Lady Liberty feel as she welcomes newcomers to America?

The Story of the Statue of Liberty

Name _____

_____

_____

_____

_____

_____

_____

_____

_____

_____

_____

Harriet's Halloween Candy

by Nancy Carlson
(1982, Carolrhoda Books, Inc.)

Harriet's Halloween bag is bulging with candy, but she still has trouble sharing her treats with baby brother Walt. In the end, Harriet learns the hard way that sharing her treats is the best way to enjoy them.

Exploring Themes of Hoarding and Sharing

❍ Ask the children how they feel about sharing. Acknowledge that sharing can be difficult. Have them tell about times they didn't want to share. Do they believe they should share everything? Why or why not?

❍ Harriet went to a lot of trouble to hide her candy. How do the students think Harriet felt when she had to put her candy in a secret place and check on it constantly? (Have students pay close attention to Harriet's facial expressions in the illustrations.) Besides getting sick of her candy, have students give other reasons why Harriet may have decided to share with Walt.

FOLLOW-UP ACTIVITIES

Hiding-Place Guessing Game

Harriet has lots of hiding places for her candy. Have fun hiding healthful treats (one per child) in secret places around the classroom. Have children search for treats. As the treats are uncovered, the children may sit down and wait for their classmates to finish their search. When everyone has a treat in hand, begin snacking. Have children describe the hiding places where they found their treats.

Candy Picture Books

Capitalize on the fact that children can easily recognize and read candy logos. Clip candy ads and coupons from magazines and newspapers. Have children identify the names of the candies featured in the print. Glue candy clippings on paper and glue pages together to create booklets. Allow space beneath glued-on clippings for children to copy the names of the candies.

Candy Lotto

Make three copies of page 31. Color all the candy on one sheet with a red crayon. Color a second sheet with a yellow crayon and a third sheet with a blue crayon. Cut these apart to create playing cards. Place cards face down in a box.

Provide each child with a copy of page 31 and three crayons (one each red, yellow, and blue). Direct students to color each candy with any one of the three colors. (Completed sheets should vary from student to student). Overturn one playing card at a time. When the overturned playing card matches the shape, size, and color of a candy piece on a student's game board, the player uses a plastic chip or a cotton ball to cover the matching candy on his or her game board. The winner is the first one to cover all of the pictures on his or her game board.

Scary, Scary Halloween

by Eve Bunting
(Clarion Books, 1986)

The vivid, scary tale captures all the delicious spookiness that is Halloween! Witches, goblins, and skeletons stalk and shock throughout the pages, but the best surprise of all is kept in the dark until the very end of the book.

Exploring Themes of Narration and Rhyme

○ Tell children that the voice telling a story is called the narrator. Ask children to decide who is telling this story. When in the story were they able to discover the narrator. Why do they think the author hid the narrator until the end of the book? How would the book be different if we knew from the beginning that the cat and kittens were telling this story?

○ Reread the book to discover the author's rhyme scheme. What scary images did the author's words conjure up? Make a list of the scary words and phrases. Hang the list in the writing corner for students to refer to when writing their own scary poems and stories.

FOLLOW-UP ACTIVITIES

Ghastly Mural

Place a length of black craft paper (cut to fit a bulletin board) on the floor. Have children dip 12-inch long pieces of yarn in white paint. Drop yarn on paper in the shape of an upside-down *u*. Lift yarn without smearing. When dry, paint yellow eyes on ghostly shapes. Staple this black paper to the bulletin board. Provide children with brown craft paper. Referring to *Scary, Scary Halloween* for inspiration, have children work together to draw large Halloween shapes and characters (pairs of eyes, leaves, pumpkins, trees, harvest moon, witches, etc.) on the paper. Paint the drawings with bright or fluorescent paints. Let dry, cut out, and arrange on ghastly mural.

Pumpkin Grins and Grimaces Graph

Provide students with orange construction paper precut into pumpkin shapes. In a box, place a supply of large and small geometric shapes (circles, squares, triangles, and rectangles), which have been precut from black construction paper. Invite students to glue shapes on their pumpkins to create a spooky jack-o'-lantern face. Then give each student a copy of page 33 on which to graph the number of shapes used when creating his or her pumpkin's face. For a class challenge, combine all the graphs into one giant graph representing *all* of the shapes used and display it with the jack-o'-lantern on the door of your classroom.

Scary, Scary Halloween

How many did you use?									
large rectangle									
small rectangle									
large square									
small square									
large triangle									
small triangle									
large circle									
small circle									
	1	2	3	4	5	6	7	8	

Thanksgiving at the Tappleton's

by Eileen Spinelli
(Addison-Wesley, 1982)

Children will love sharing in the hilarious mishaps that prevent the Tappleton's traditional Thanksgiving feast from making it to the table. But, the silly (and unfortunate) turn of events can't dampen this clan's ability to celebrate the true meaning of Thanksgiving.

Exploring Themes of Fun and Family

❍ Mrs. Tappleton sinks the Thanksgiving turkey in a pond, but tells her husband that the reason he can't smell the bird cooking is because he has a cold. Mr. Tappleton arrives at the bakery too late to buy any pies for dessert, so he returns home with two empty boxes tied with string. He tells his wife that the boxes feel light because the pies are so light. How do the children feel about the characters fibbing to each other? How do these fibs contribute to the book's silly story line? If this were a true story, would these things happen the same way? Why or why not?

❍ In the conclusion of the book, the Tappletons realize that the true meaning of Thanksgiving lies not in the feast, but in the family. Ask students to talk about the meaning of family. Ask them to think of the word *family* in a new way. Introduce the idea of the "extended family," which may include friends and relations outside the immediate family. Talk about other types of "family," which may develop in the classroom and in the community. Help the children to understand a family as a group of people (who may or may not be related) who care about each other.

FOLLOW-UP ACTIVITIES

Classroom Family Tree

Make a classroom family tree. Insert a real tree branch into a large mason jar. Surround the branch with clear marbles or soil. Collect photos of children (or reproduce children's individual class photos on a copy machine). Have children make leaves by tracing their hands (fingers together) on construction paper. Cut out and glue pictures onto hands. Punch holes in palms of hands. Thread ribbon or yard through hole and hang leaves (fingers down) from the branches of the tree.

Fine-Feathered Thanksgiving Turkey

Have children talk about what they are thankful for. Record their answers on a large chart pad. Distribute copies of page 35. Have children trace turkey parts on shades of brown and yellow construction paper (they may trace as many feathers as they wish) and cut them out. Invite children to write something they are thankful for on each feather. (Refer to the chart pad for inspiration.) Glue feathers, feet, and head to a circle of construction paper or small paper plate as shown in the illustration. Glue turkey onto colorful construction-paper background (red or orange works well). Have children share their creations with the group.

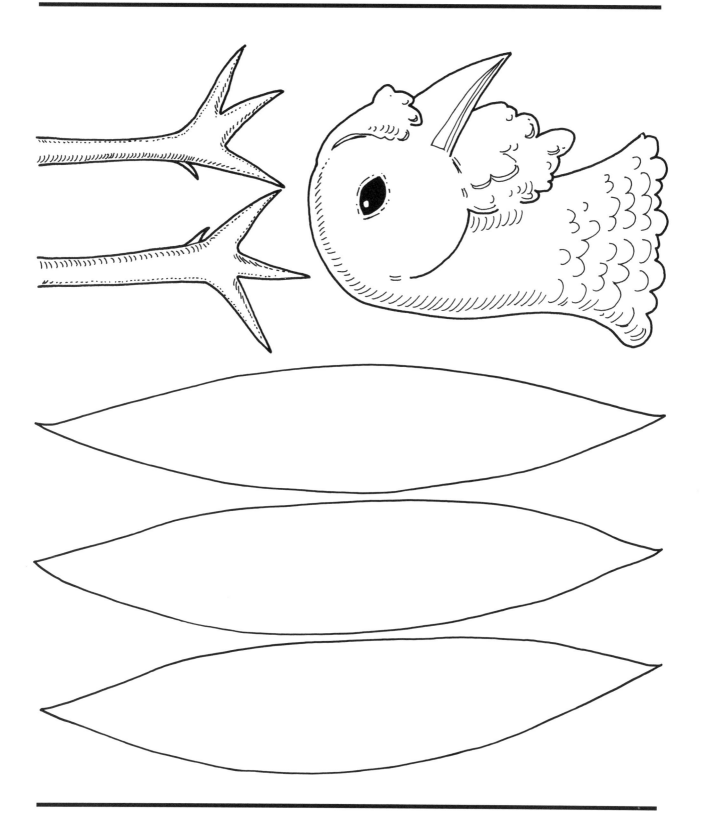

Sarah Morton's Day

by Kate Waters
(Scholastic, 1989)

Readers are treated to a touching, realistic view of Pilgrim life as seen through the eyes of nine-year-old Sarah Morton. Photographed in full color at Plymouth Plantation, a living history museum in Plymouth, Massachusetts, Sarah Morton's Day helps readers understand what it meant to be a Pilgrim girl in 1627.

Exploring Themes of the Pilgrim Days and Pilgrim Dress

○ After reading *Sarah Morton's Day*, have children decide what part of Sarah's day is similar or different from their own. Have them make a list of similarities and differences. Which list has more items? Draw children's attention to the glossary in the back of the book. Which words or phrases have changed? Which ones are no longer used at all because our lifestyles have changed?

○ Look at the pictures showing Sarah putting on her overgarments. Ask the children to count how many pieces of clothing (overgarments) they usually wear. How would they feel if they wore Sarah's clothes each day?

FOLLOW-UP ACTIVITIES

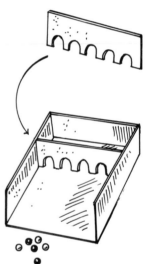

Knicker Box Game

Begin with a large cardboard box. Using a craft knife, cut off one end of the lid. On the piece cut from the lid, draw five arches, each large enough to allow a marble to pass through. Using packing tape, secure this piece into the box, about two-thirds of the way from the open end (as illustrated). Let children take turn trying to roll marbles through the arches.

Cornbread for Your Midday Meal

Preheat oven to 425°
Grease 9-by-9-inch pan

Sift together:

³/₄ cup all purpose flour
2¹/₂ tsp. baking powder
1 Tbl. sugar
1¹/₄ cups yellow corn meal

In separate bowl combine:

one egg, beaten
2 Tbl. melted butter
1 cup milk

Combine liquid and dry ingredients; pour into pan and bake for 25 to 30 min.

"My Day" Books

Sarah Morton's Day is a look at one day in the life of a Pilgrim girl. Provide students with copies of page 37 and ask them to keep track of how they spend their days. After gathering this information for a few days, have students write "My Day" books patterned after the dawn-to-dusk format of *Sarah Morton's Day*. Have students illustrate their books with original drawings or photographs.

Daily Time Log
How I spend my day

(1/2 hour intervals)

6:00 a.m. _____

6:30 a.m. _____

7:00 a.m. _____

7:30 a.m. _____

8:00 a.m. _____

8:30 a.m. _____

9:00 a.m. _____

9:30 a.m. _____

10:00 a.m. _____

10:30 a.m. _____

11:00 a.m. _____

11:30 a.m. _____

12:00 p.m. _____

12:30 p.m. _____

1:00 p.m. _____

1:30 p.m. _____

2:00 p.m. _____

2:30 p.m. _____

3:00 p.m. _____

3:30 p.m. _____

4:00 p.m. _____

4:30 p.m. _____

5:00 p.m. _____

5:30 p.m. _____

6:00 p.m. _____

6:30 p.m. _____

7:00 p.m. _____

7:30 p.m. _____

8:00 p.m. _____

8:30 p.m. _____

9:00 p.m. _____

9:30 p.m. _____

10:00 p.m. _____

10:30 p.m. _____

11:00 p.m. _____

Johnny Appleseed

retold by Stephen Kellogg
(William Morrow, 1988)

In recounting and illustrating the life of Johnny Appleseed, Stephen Kellogg helps young learners understand how stories of Johnny's life often became exaggerated and embellished. Kellogg also helps children appreciate how such stories can keep a beloved legend alive and influential long after his death.

Exploring Themes of Riches and Exaggerations

❍ Johnny believed he "lived like a king in his wilderness home," and so he resisted suggestions that he settle down and build a house. Ask children how it was that Johnny felt like royalty. He didn't have a crown or jewels or money or people to rule. Why wasn't Johnny uncomfortable, unhappy, or worried?

❍ Ask: How were people's stories of Johnny a good example of exaggeration? Why did people claim Johnny was stronger, kinder, or smarter than he was? Research the exaggeration surrounding other heroes and legends (for example, Finn M'Coul, Paul Bunyan, Daniel Boone, Robin Hood, etc.).

FOLLOW-UP ACTIVITIES

Apples in Language and Literature

Share apple tales with students. Tell the story of Snow White or William Tell. Ask children to find out what is meant by the following:

- apple-pie order
- the apple of my eye
- an apple a day keeps the doctor away

Create Superheroes

Help students draw comparisons between the legend of Johnny Appleseed and modern-day superheroes. Have children talk about their favorite superheroes. What powers do the heroes possess? Have the children realize that superpowers need not be violent. Have children talk about powers they might like to possess. These may include the ability to fly, the power to move heavy objects, and the power to see through objects.

Help children trace their bodies on craft paper. Have them paint themselves in superhero costumes. Have them list their superpowers and how these powers may be used to help others. Attach these lists to the paper heroes and display for all to enjoy.

Apple Fest Recipe Book

Give each student a copy of page 39. Have them use the page to record favorite apple recipes. Make copies of each recipe and bind into cookbooks for the class. Plan an applefest. Have children make their recipes at home and bring them to school on the day of the feast.

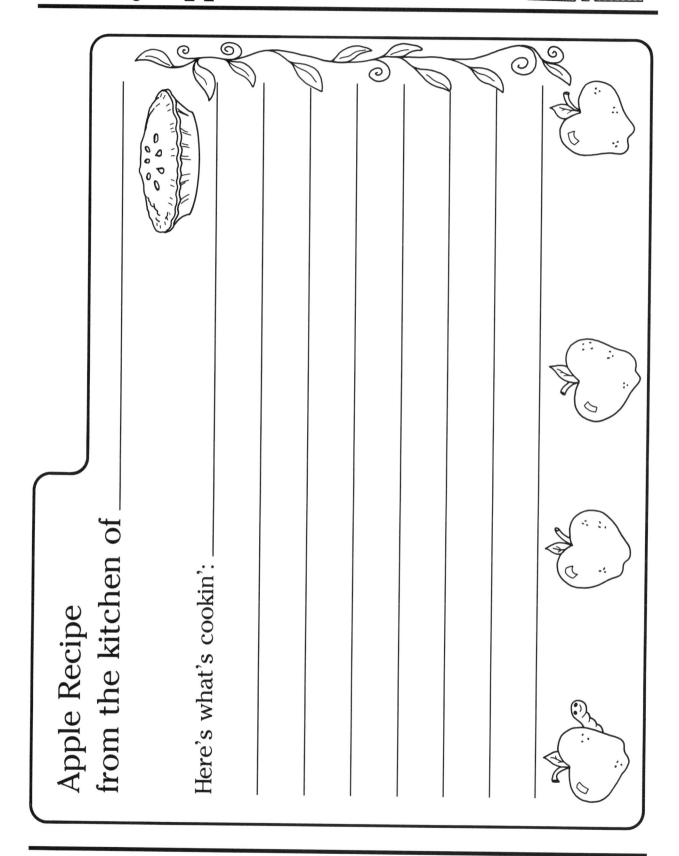

Apple Recipe
from the kitchen of _____

Here's what's cookin':

Johnny Appleseed

by Jan Gleiter and Kathleen Thompson
(Raintree Publishers, Inc. 1987)

This book faithfully recounts the story of John Chapman, otherwise known as Johnny Appleseed. With a batchful of seeds and a heartful of love, Johnny is shown spreading apples and sunshine across a young America. The warm pictures and text will open children to the book's simple message: Because of one special man, the world is a better place.

Exploring Themes of Happiness and Heroics

○ Johnny Appleseed lived a rich life, even though he was poor, had no home, and owned very few things. Ask the children how it is possible that Johnny Appleseed was so happy without owning money and things.

○ Look in a dictionary and find the definitions of the following words: *hero, legend,* and *legacy*. How is Johnny Appleseed both a hero and a legend? Heroes perform acts of courage. What brave or courageous acts did Johnny perform? Are the stories about Johnny fact or fiction? What was Johnny's legacy to us?

FOLLOW-UP ACTIVITIES

Apple Books

Give each child seven copies of page 41 (one for the front cover, one for the back cover, and five for the book's pages). Help complete pages as directed below, or dream up your own apple-inspired ideas!

○ Page One: Slice apples in half horizontally. Show children how to dip apples in non-toxic red paint. (Blot on newspaper.) Press on page to create prints.

○ Page Two: Have class collect apple seeds. Tell children to draw a picture of Johnny Appleseed planting seeds in the ground. Then have them glue real seeds on picture to make illustration look more realistic.

○ Page Three: Have students sample, record, and illustrate a favorite apple recipe or product (apple pie, applesauce, apple butter, apple cake, apple muffins, etc.). How many different uses for apples can students find?

○ Page Four: Challenge children to research apple varieties (Red Delicious, Golden Delicious, Granny Smith, Rome, etc.), then list the names of as many apple varieties as they can.

○ Page Five: Work with students to create a series of apple similes such as: Apples are as red as _____, or Apples are crunchy as _____. Brainstorm and use a large chart pad to record your ideas. Transfer your "simile poem" onto a copy of page 41. Reproduce enough copies of the poem for the whole class. Have students paste a copy of this group poem onto page five of their books.

After the books' pages are complete, invite students to decorate the covers of their apple books and think of delicious titles!

Apple Tree Bulletin Board

Cover a bulletin board with sky-blue paper. Paint a large apple tree trunk on the covered board or cut a large tree shape from brown craft paper and staple it to the board. Hang apple books (see activity above) on the tree branches.

Winter Celebrations

Harriet and Walt

by Nancy Carlson
(Carolrhoda Books, 1982)

Yippie! Harriet can't wait to go out and play in the snow—that is until her mother says little brother Walt must tag along. As Harriet fears, baby Walt spoils all the fun. But when Walt takes a scary tumble, Harriet begins treating the little guy with all the patience and love only a big sister can offer—and the winter fun is saved!

Exploring Themes of Cold Winter Fun and Warm Caring Ways

❍ Harriet can't wait to play in the snow! Have children reread the book and make a list of how Harriet plays in the snow. Add the children's own snow games to the list.

❍ Why does Harriet grumble when she has to babysit for Walt? What happens when Walt tries to play with Harriet and George? Encourage children to describe times they had to play with older or younger playmates. What made the playtime fun or miserable?

FOLLOW-UP ACTIVITIES

Soap-Flake Snowpeople

Using a manual or electric mixer, whip soap flakes and water together in a large bowl until they have the consistency of very stiff whipped cream. On the wrong (dull) side of finger-paint paper, draw snowpeople outlines to desired sizes (at least 12 inches tall). Turn paper over. Spritz shiny side of paper with water from a spray bottle (or sprinkle water on with fingertips). Place approximately 1/2 cup of soap mixture on the moistened paper. Have children finger paint with the mixture. Encourage children to pretend their fingers are playing in snow. Fingers may slip, slide, hop, run, and drag through the mixture. When paintings dry, turn over and cut out snowpeople shapes. These may be decorated (on the snowy side) with features cut from construction paper or wallpaper sample books.

Winter Dress-up Game

Provide each player with one die and a copy of page 45. Draw players' attention to the number-coded clothing key at the bottom of the page. Tell players that the number on the die will determine what clothing piece they may add to their dog. (Students may draw a line to connect clothing to the dog or they may put clothing directly on the dog.) At any time, players may roll the die twice, add the scores together, and use this sum to determine which clothing piece may be added to their dog. (Rolling the die twice does not enable a player to add two pieces of clothing to his or her dog.) The player who dresses the dog first is the winner. (For a noncompetitive version of this game, players work as a team and keep track of the number of rolls needed to dress the dog. Players may play the game repeatedly, working together to dress dog in the least number of turns possible.)

Owl Moon

Owl Pouch Pattern

Cut one
yellow felt

front of
pouch

Cut one
brown felt

back of
pouch

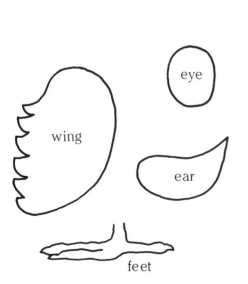

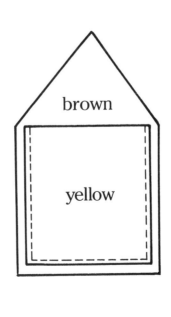

finished pouch

Angelina's Christmas

by Katharine Holabird
(Crown, 1985)

Tiny Angelina mouse reveals her lion-sized heart when she shows concern for a elderly neighbor mouse who must spend Christmas alone. The author cleverly spins a "story within a story" as the neighbor mouse, Mr. Bell, recounts his surprising Christmases of bygone times.

Exploring Themes of Lonely Hearts and Heartfelt Surprises

❍ Angelina doesn't want Mr. Bell to feel lonely on Christmas, so she prepares some holiday treats for him. Ask the children how they can tell if someone is feeling sad or lonely. Is feeling lonely the same thing as feeling sad? Brainstorm ideas for helping someone in need have a happy holiday season, and then talk about other year-round ideas that can help chase away the blues.

❍ Mr. Bell surprises Angelina and Henry by dressing up as Santa. Have students recall surprises they received that didn't come from a store. List these surprises on a large chart pad. Transfer the list to individual pieces of paper. Have each child illustrate his or her own contribution. Bind pages together to make a class collaborative entitled "Heartfelt Surprises."

FOLLOW-UP ACTIVITIES

Mouse Stand-Up Greeting Cards

Reproduce and cut out medium-sized mouse pattern on page 49. Fold gray, white, or light brown construction paper accordion style creating 4 wide strips. Place mouse pattern on folded paper and cut around edge of shape being careful not to trim folded edges of the paper completely away. Unfold paper to reveal connected chain of mice. Use markers, construction paper, fabric scraps, lace trim, cotton balls, and glitter to decorate mice to resemble characters in *Angelina's Christmas*.

A Puppet Show Surprise

Surprise other classes and family members with a puppet rendition of *Angelina's Christmas*. Reproduce the mouse patterns on page 49. Place patterns on pieces of gray, white, and tan construction paper. (Large pattern may be used to make adult characters, medium pattern may be used to make Angelina and her friends, and small pattern may be used to make Henry.) For each puppet, cut two matching pattern pieces from the same colored paper. Glue a wooden craft stick between these two pieces. Let dry and decorate with markers, construction paper, fabric scraps, lace trim, cotton balls, and glitter. Add yarn tail and pipe-cleaner whiskers. As the story is read or retold, puppets may be used to speak for the characters.

glue
two together

wooden
craft stick

Angelina's Christmas

Chita's Christmas Tree

by Elizabeth Fitzgerald Howard
(Bradbury Press, 1989)

Set in turn-of-the-century Baltimore, Chita's Christmas Tree *is a tale of joy and anticipation. Central to the story is a little girl's longing for a perfect deep green pine tree—"the loveliest tree in the woods." Chita's family celebration evokes all the warmth and security of a childhood Christmas worth remembering—and a tree worth waiting for!*

Exploring Themes of Olden Days and Timeless Hopes

❍ Have students take a second look at *Chita's Christmas Tree.* What clues in the story and illustrations tells us that it takes place long ago? How would the story be the same or different today?

❍ *Chita's Christmas Tree* is filled with secrets and surprises, both big and small. Ask: What secret do Chita and her father share with Henry the horse? What secret does Chita share with her mother? What surprise does Chita find Christmas morning? Tell how secrets and surprises are an important part of many other celebrations throughout the year (birthdays, anniversaries, Hanukkah, Halloween, Valentine's Day, etc.). Have children take turns telling stories of successful surprises they planned.

FOLLOW-UP ACTIVITIES

Cinnamony Christmas Waffle Recipe

Sift together:

1³/₄ cup cake flour
2 tsp. baking powder
pinch salt
1 tsp. cinnamon

Beat together:

1¹/₂ cups milk
3 egg yolks (reserve whites)
¹/₄ cup melted butter

Pour liquid ingredients into dry ingredients. Batter will be slightly lumpy. Beat egg whites until stiff and fold gently into batter. Ladle batter onto hot waffle iron grid and cook each waffle for approximately four minutes, or until waffle doesn't stick to iron.

Pine Tree Stencil Scenes

Give each student a copy of page 51, green contruction paper, white paint, and a sponge square with a clothespin attached. Have students cut out tree stencils and place where desired on green paper. Then they dip sponges into the paint, blot on newspaper, and dab paint where the stencil touches the paper. Lift stencils away. Let dry. If desired, add woodland details (animals, people, etc.) with markers.

Holiday Tree Ornaments

Trace stencil shapes on page 51 onto green oaktag. Cut out, punch a hole in top of ornament and slip yarn through hole. Decorate with markers. Brush with a wash of white glue and water. Dip into translucent glitter (sold in craft stores). Hang to dry.

Malke's Secret Recipe

by David A. Adler
(Kar-Ben Copies, 1989)

Malke makes the softest, lightest potato pancakes (latkes) in the town of Chelm, but her recipe is a secret. Berel the shoemaker holds deliciously fond memories of Malke's latkes. He decides to steal and recreate Malke's recipe, but doesn't count on his wife's jealous interference.

Exploring Themes of Memories and Jealousy

○ Malke's latkes tasted "even better in people's memories than they had tasted on their forks." Ask the children to tell what they think this statement means. Are we always able to remember things exactly as they were? Why or why not?

○ Reread the book and look carefully at the way the illustrator depicted Yentel. How is Yentel feeling as Berel tries to make Malke's latke recipe? Brainstorm some possible reasons for her feelings.

FOLLOW-UP ACTIVITIES

Memorable Latkes

Use Malke's recipe in the back of the book, or follow this recipe: Grate 2 cups mature potatoes and blot with paper towels to absorb excess moisture. Place potatoes in a large bowl. Add three beaten eggs. Sift together 1½ tablespoons flour and a pinch of salt and add to potato mixture. Add 2 teaspoons grated onion. Stir mixture together and shape into pancake-size patties. Fry in hot safflower oil. Blot again to remove grease. Serve latkes hot with applesauce, sour cream, or plain yogurt.

Visual Memory Cooking Game

After making latkes with the class, review the names and functions of the cooking tools used in the process (spoons, bowl, grater, egg beater or whisk, spatula, etc.). Place tools on a table and cover with a cloth. Have children take turns hiding their eyes while you remove one tool from the table. Have children look again at the selection of tools and guess which is missing.

Family Food Booklets

Give each student several copies of page 53. Have children work with parents or other adults in the family to discover and record which recipes have been "in the family for generations." (Have families include some easy recipes that you may try making in class.) Encourage children to discover ethnic origins of the recipes. Staple each student's completed pages together to form cook booklets. Booklet covers may be made by gluing an extra copy of page 53 on construction paper and asking children to draw themselves cooking or eating one of their own recipe selections. Have children share their books with the class. If possible, have children bring in samples of their recipes for the group to sample, or consider making the recipes in class.

Malke's Secret Recipe

Recipe for _____

From the kitchen of _____

Here I am tasting _____

The Odd Potato

by Eileen Sherman
(Kar-Ben Copies, 1984)

Rachel wants to celebrate Hanukkah, but her dad, Mr. Levy, lost interest in holidays since his wife's death 18 months earlier. Rachel realizes that if a celebration is to take place, it will be up to her. How Rachel's Hanukkah celebration manages to pull her family together is a touching tribute to childhood, families, and tradition.

Exploring Themes of Memories and "Making Do"

❍ Reread *The Odd Potato*. Look again at the illustrations of Rachel's dad. Ask: How does he look since his wife's death? Imagine what he thinks about. Why doesn't he help Rachel find the family menorah when she first asks him? What changes his mind?

❍ When Rachel gives up trying to locate the family menorah, she concentrates on making potato latkes. When she can only get hold of one gnarled potato, she isn't disappointed or discouraged. Instead, she continues to make the most of what she has. Draw students' attention to Rachel's indomitable spirit. How would the story be different if Rachel had given up trying to have a Hanukkah celebration? If she had given up, how would her father and brother have felt during Hanukkah? Were latkes and a pretty menorah the most important part of the celebration? If not, what was the most important part of the celebration?

FOLLOW-UP ACTIVITIES

Potato Menorah

Have each child bring a large potato to class. Using a fork (or a nail), pierce eight holes in each potato, plus one extra hole for the *shamash* or "leader" candle. Secure a small candle into each hole.

Gift Box

Have children collect department store boxes with lids. Cut drawing paper to fit in the bottom of each box. Have children draw a special gift they would like to receive (as much as Rachel wanted her father to find the family menorah). Encourage children to illustrate gifts that cannot be bought at the store. Cover box lids with sheets of newspaper comics and decorate with recycled bows. Tack boxes to bulletin board. Place lids on boxes and create hinge by taping lid to box along top side. Complete bulletin board display with the heading, "Gift Wrapped Wishes."

Traditionally Speaking

Have students use copies of page 55 to research and record holiday traditions they celebrate with their families. Have children write and illustrate stories about their most memorable holiday traditions.

The Odd Potato

Our Holiday Traditions

Holiday _____

Preparations _____

_____

_____

Who we celebrate with _____

_____

_____

Surprises we plan _____

_____

_____

Food we eat _____

_____

_____

Ceremonies we take part in _____

_____

_____

_____

Our Martin Luther King Book

by Patricia McKissack
(The Child's World, Inc. 1986)

Here we join teacher Mrs. Stevens and her inquisitive students as they learn about the history and life of Martin Luther King, Jr. As the children in the book participate in a variety of activities designed to help them understand and appreciate King's work, we are inspired to do the same.

Exploring Themes of Civil Rights, Responsibilities, and Freedom

❍ Look in a dictionary to find definitions for *civil* and *rights*. Talk with the class about the civil rights depicted on the poster Mrs. Stevens and her class created. Copy these rights on a chart pad. Help the children add to the list. Your list might include the right to worship as we choose, the right to free speech, the right to own property, etc.

❍ Ask children to tell what they know about the word *freedom*. Does being free mean being able to do whatever you want whenever you want? Why or why not?

FOLLOW-UP ACTIVITIES

Blue Circles/Yellow Circles

Tell children that this activity will help them understand what it feels like to be discriminated against. Divide the class in half. Pin blue construction-paper circles on half of the group and yellow construction-paper circles on the other half. Allow only children with the blue circles to enjoy certain free-choice privileges such as walking first in line, playing games while others work, having first chance at choosing learning centers or playground equipment, or having a homework-free night. Then, allow only the children with the yellow circles to enjoy the privileges. (Limit this exercise to a specific length of time or for the duration of a specific activity and inform children when you plan to begin and end the activity.) Talk with the children about how they felt when they were allowed freedoms as opposed to how they felt when they were left out or treated unfairly. Ask them to imagine how they would feel if they lived a lifetime of being treated unfairly. What would they do about their feelings? What would they do to change the situation?

Martin Luther King Sequence Book

Provide children with copies of page 57 and help them read the words. Brainstorm possible illustration ideas for each frame. Illustrate. Clip frames apart and arrange in correct sequence to form a booklet. Have children read their booklets to each other and their families.

Our Martin Luther King Book

for I have a dream . . . .

Martin Luther King, Jr. is born on January 15, 1929.

Martin reads and studies about peace. He becomes a preacher.

Martin marries Coretta. They move to Montgomery and try to help end unjust laws.

In April 1968, Martin is assassinated. Today we celebrate his memory by keeping his dream of love, peace, and justice alive.

Martin Luther King Day

by Linda Lowery
(Carolrhoda Books, 1987)

January 20, 1986, was the first celebration of a new holiday in the history of the United States: Martin Luther King Day. This book commemorates the history of a man who shared and lived his dream of peace, equality, and freedom for all people.

Exploring Themes of Courage and Equality

❍ As a boy, Martin Luther King, Jr., experienced prejudice and inequality. When he grew up he decided he would try to change things. Ask children how they feel when unfair things happen to them. How else could Martin have reacted? Why did Martin need courage to help make the world a better place?

❍ Look up the word *prejudice* in the dictionary. Help children understand that the word *prejudice* means to prejudge without full knowledge. Inform students that the word *prejudice* is often used when talking about a negative racial or cultural bias. Talk about the phrase, "judging a book by its cover." Ask the children to share times they had an opinion about someone or something by looks alone (children often prejudge food based on the way it looks). Discuss whether these prejudgments were proven right or wrong.

FOLLOW-UP ACTIVITIES

Historic Time Line

Draw a horizontal line on a paper-covered bulletin board. Have children trace their hands on construction paper. Cut several hands from each pattern. Mark the line's endpoints to represent the years of Martin Luther King's life. Have children research the highlights of King's life. Use hand shapes to record highlights. Attach hands at appropriate places on the time line. Have children record their own ideas for promoting peace and equality. Attach these hands around the time line. Finish board with the title: "Martin Luther King, Jr., Taught Us to Reach for Peace."

Judge a Book by Its Cover

Provide students with copies of page 59 and photos or pictures of people you are familiar with, but they won't recognize. (These photos may be of famous personalities, political figures, etc.) Have children use page 59 to record information about the person in the picture. (This information will be generated solely on the basis of the people's appearance.) Attach photo or picture to the biography. Using additional copies of page 59, record actual biographical information about each person pictured. Read these and have the whole class try to match the description to the picture. After the actual photo identities have been revealed, have students share how closely their imagined biographies matched the real profiles. Ask the children what they learned from this exercise. Have they ever judged someone before really knowing them? Is this a fair practice?

Martin Luther King Day

Person's Name _____

Person's Occupation _____

Person's Age (optional) _____

Describe this person's home _____

_____

_____

Person's Interests and Hobbies _____

_____

_____

Person's Habits _____

_____

Person's Likes and Dislikes _____

_____

Person's Language _____

Amount of Education _____

Describe this person's family _____

_____

Compiled by _____

Louanne Pig and the Mysterious Valentine

by Nancy Carlson
(Carolrhoda Books, 1985)

Louanne Pig receives a beautiful Valentine's Day card, but can't figure out who sent it. Her only clue is that the sender signed the card with a green pen. As the story ends, Louanne is still baffled about the mystery while observant readers know all!

Exploring Themes of Curiosity and Satisfaction

❍ Talk about curiosity. What does it mean to be curious? Ask: Have you ever felt as curious as Louanne? If you received a secret valentine, would you do the things Louanne did to find out who sent it?

❍ When the book ends, Louanne Pig hasn't solved her mystery, but careful readers know the answer. When a mystery is solved it's very *satisfying* to the reader. Why did the author allow us to solve the mystery? After Louanne says, "I wonder if I'll get one [valentine] next year," what happens? Write and illustrate a new ending to the book. This time, have Louanne solve the mystery of her valentine.

FOLLOW-UP ACTIVITIES

Mystery Valentines

Print students' names on individual slips of paper. Place in a shoe box and let children select names at random. Next, using crayons, markers, construction paper, glitter, glue, and scissors, have students create valentines and then secretly send them. Invite children to guess who sent their valentines.

Day-by-Day Calendar Surprises

With this calendar activity, children will be able to enjoy a daily valentine surprise from their classmates. At the beginning of the month, give each child two copies of page 61. On one copy, help them cut the doors open along the dotted lines. Then glue or staple the clipped calendar page over an intact calendar page and mount calendars on colorful construction paper. Have children sit in a circle with their calendars and crayons or markers. Beginning with the box marking the first day of the month, have children open the door and draw a tiny valentine in the empty space. Then have children pass the calendar to the next person who will illustrate the space behind the second door. Continue rotating and drawing until the calendars have been completely illustrated. Smooth doors shut. Have children work on their own calendars to fill in the dates on the doors. Each day, open a door to reveal the surprise illustration there. (This activity may be repeated to celebrate any month.)

Louanne Pig and the Mysterious Valentine

Month	Sunday	Monday	Tuesday	Wednesday	Thursday	Friday	Saturday

Arthur's Valentine

by Marc Brown
(Little Brown and Co., 1980)

When a "secret admirer" begins sending valentines and love notes to Arthur, he also receives a lot of teasing from his friends. But when Arthur manages to solve the mystery, he plans a secret valentine surprise of his own.

Exploring Themes of Teasing and Secrets

❍ When Arthur's friends learn about his "secret admirer," they make fun of him. They sing teasing songs and chant teasing rhymes. Ask the class why the others treat Arthur this way. How does the teasing make Arthur feel? How do they know? Have children recount times they were teased and how they reacted.

❍ Hold a discussion about secrets. What are secrets? Are secrets bad or good? What secrets took place in *Arthur's Valentine*? When was Arthur secretive? Why did he plan such a secret?

FOLLOW-UP ACTIVITIES

Valentine Mailboxes

For each mailbox you will need: one shoe box, a large piece (11 by 14 inches) of construction paper (pink, white, or violet), assorted sizes of hearts cut from construction paper, holiday stickers, glue, tape, and doilies (optional). Glue or tape construction paper to shoe box as shown in illustration. Decorate with doilies, hearts, and stickers. Mailbox is ready to receive, transport, and store valentine deliveries.

Valentine "Kiss" Cookies

Make your favorite peanut-butter cookie recipe. One minute before baking time is up, pull cookie trays from oven and press a chocolate kiss into each cookie. Return tray to oven and allow heat to slightly melt chocolate kiss into cookie.

Valentine Rebus Cards

Explain to students that a rebus is a message written with pictures instead of words. Practice this technique by substituting rebus pictures for some of the words in Arthur's valentines. Then provide students with pink or white construction paper and copies of page 63. Have children identify the words represented by the pictures then make up some of their own. Record these on a chart pad and display in the writing center. Have children pick classmates' names from a hat, then use page 63 and the class chart to prepare secret rebus valentines for each other. Share the valentines and try to guess who sent each card.

Arthur's Valentine

I   be   honey

heart
(or love)   kiss   sweet

to   you   you
(ewe)

happy   time

George Washington: Father of Our Country

by David A. Adler
(Holiday House, 1988)

This book is among a series of "first biographies" by the author. It recounts the life of George Washington from his boyhood through his presidency. The book portrays Washington as a man who fought for freedom while rejecting both power and wealth.

Exploring the Theme of Leadership

○ George Washington spent most of his life leading others. Ask: What does it mean to be a leader? Do leaders always need followers? Why or why not? (Have children offer examples from their own lives when they've been called on to lead others—perhaps they've been expected to show a good example for siblings.) What are the best parts about being a leader? What are some difficult parts? Have children explain why Washington was different from the leaders (i.e. royalty) he was used to following.

> ### FOLLOW-UP ACTIVITIES

If I Ran for the Presidency

George Washington was elected our first president because people believed he was a good problem solver. Have children imagine they want to be elected President of the United States. What would their responsibilities and powers be as president? Have the class brainstorm problems to be addressed in the country, record responses on the board, and then have each child copy the list according to his or her personal priorities. Then, have students write campaign speeches designed to win voter support based on their proposed solutions to the problems.

Follow the Leaders

Discuss with the class why good leaders are important. Help them to understand that "following a leader" can mean many things from following specific advice to trying to copy a role model. Provide each student with a copy of page 65. Have children think of leaders they know in their own lives. The list should include famous figures as well as leaders from their personal lives. Remind children that their lists will vary because we each have special people we choose to follow. Then have students brainstorm the qualities a good leader needs, such as intelligence, fairness, gentility, dependability, likability, strength, sensitivity, etc. You may need to label the qualities the children describe. (When thinking of qualities, it may help students to think of special talents and traits their own leaders have in common.)

Have each child choose one leader from the list and describe why that person is particularly important or influential in his or her life. Finally, invite children to tell of a time when they led others. How did it feel to be a leader? Encourage students to explain why they think it's more fun to be a leader or a follower.

George Washington

Leaders I know . . .

_____
_____
_____
_____
_____
_____

Leadership qualities:

_____
_____
_____
_____
_____
_____

I was a leader when . . .

_____
_____
_____
_____
_____
_____

Abraham Lincoln: President of a Divided Country

by Carol Green
(Children's Press, 1989)

This biography of Abraham Lincoln, 16th president of the United States, follows his life from boyhood to death. Photos, sketches, and illustrations help bring Lincoln and his story to life. The text itself is simple enough for young readers to appreciate, while detailed enough to fascinate.

Exploring Themes of Hardships and Literacy

❍ Lincoln faced many sad and difficult times in his life. List some of these on a chart pad or chalkboard. Ask children to describe how Lincoln may have felt during each of these times. Do the students think Lincoln's feelings helped him understand the sadness of slaves? How?

❍ Search *Abraham Lincoln* for illustrations of Lincoln enjoying books. Have students hypothesize about why reading was so important to him. How did reading help Lincoln achieve his goals? Have students hunt for evidence that Lincoln passed on his love of reading to his children.

FOLLOW-UP ACTIVITIES

Log-Cabin Banks

Have each child measure the dimensions of a small milk carton. Cut tan construction paper to fit the carton and then glue it on. Glue strips of brown construction paper (approximately half an inch wide) to the carton to resemble logs. Add construction paper door, windows, and roof. With craft knife, cut a slit in the roof to put money through.

Lincoln Bookmark

Reminded children of Lincoln's love of reading with this bookmark project. Begin by distributing sheets of thin copy paper. (Paper with print on one side is okay). Place a bunch of pennies on a table. Lay papers (print side down) over the pennies. Gently rub the paper with the side of a copper- or brown-colored crayon until the image of Lincoln appears. Cut the papers into rectangles (2½-by-5 inches) with pinking shears. Glue the rectangles (allowing 1-inch margins between each) onto brown construction paper. Laminate. Trim apart with pinking shears. Punch a hole in the top of each bookmark, thread brown yarn through and knot.

Letters to Lincoln

Abraham Lincoln faced many difficult times and decisions in his lifetime. He was also noted for loving and listening to children. Pretend that you and your students lived in Lincoln's lifetime. Have each student use a copy of page 67 to compose a letter to Lincoln to help him through a difficult time in his life. Here are some ideas:

- Lincoln's life as a poor child
- Lincoln's anger about slavery and his feelings towards people who hated him
- Lincoln's concerns about the Civil War

Abraham Lincoln

Date _____

Dear Mr. Lincoln:

_____

_____

_____

_____

_____

_____

_____

Sincerely,

_____

Jeremy Bean's St. Patrick's Day

by Alice Schertle
(Lothrop, Lee & Shepard Books, 1987)

Jeremy Bean looks forward to going to school on St. Patrick's Day. But when Jeremy forgets to wear his green sweater to school, he is teased by the other kids and ends up hiding in the broom closet. In a surprise ending, a special friend rescues Jeremy and helps him to celebrate St. Patrick's Day in style.

Exploring Themes of Fear and Forgetfulness

❍ Jeremy Bean was fearful of the principal. Ask the children to relate stories of people they once feared, but now they are comfortable being around. What helped to change their feelings? Do our fears ever serve a good purpose (such as protecting us from strangers)?

❍ Jeremy's troubles began when he forgot to wear his green sweater on St. Patrick's Day. Have children describe times their forgetfulness got them into trouble or created a problem for them. Brainstorm some ways to avoid forgetfulness. Record these on a large chart pad and post as memory reminders.

FOLLOW-UP ACTIVITIES

Pin the Green on Jeremy Bean

Have one student lay down on a length of craft paper. Trace around the student's body. Paint to resemble Jeremy Bean. Cut out the paper Jeremy and hang on the wall, bulletin board, or door. Then, provide students with bow ties cut from green paper. Attach a rolled piece of masking tape to each tie. Blindfold students, turn them around three times, and have try to "pin" the bow tie on Jeremy Bean. The student who comes closest wins.

Musical Top Hat

Make a top hat from green construction paper. Have children sit in a circle. Play Irish music and have students pass the hat around. One child controls when the music stops (but he or she is not able to see the circle of children). When the music stops, the child holding the hat operates the recorder or record player. The last child to hold the hat becomes the first child to operate the music in the next game.

Stitch a Flag for a Parade

In Ireland, children carry flags and march in parades to commemorate St. Patrick's Day. And Ireland is famous for its stitchery. So use the pattern on page 69 to help students stitch the Irish flag. Use running stitch to appliqué green, white, and orange felt rectangles to the sides of a full piece of felt. (Use overhand stitch to fasten felt flags to small wooden dowels (or glue in place) and have children hold flags as they march around the classroom to Irish marching music.

Jeremy Bean's
St. Patrick's Day

Cut two
GREEN
felt.

Cut two
WHITE
felt.

Cut two
ORANGE
felt.

Cut one full piece of any color felt.

Fin M'Coul

Retold and Illustrated by Tomie dePaola
(Holiday House, 1981)

The Irish folktale of giant Fin M'Coul comes to life in this delightful book. Written in a lilting, lyrical style, the book speaks of strength, fear, and loyalty. And the story's resolution even sparkles with a bit of Irish magic.

Exploring Themes of Fear and the Power of Peaceful Resolution

❍ Fins M'Coul is a strong giant with giant-sized fears. Ask children how it is possible for Fin to be fearful and strong at the same time? Have children support their ideas with examples from their own experiences.

❍ Fin's wife, Oonagh, "fights" Cucullin by tricking him. Discuss the power of peaceful resolution. Can students cite other examples of peaceful resolution? Can they explain how peaceful solutions can involve a special kind of power? Some people believe that fighting is the most powerful way to solve a problem. Do students agree? Have them offer support for their opinions.

FOLLOW-UP ACTIVITIES

Braided Good-Luck Bracelets

Oonagh braids yarn into bracelets as part of a fairy charm. Your students can do the same and exchange the bracelets as a gesture of friendship and luck. Give each student three pieces (8 inches long) of thin yarn. Knot strands together at one end, braid, and knot the other end. Tie bracelets around students' wrists or ankles.

Retell *Fin M'Coul* as a Modern-Day Tale

Have students work together to retell the story of Fin M'Coul in their own words, in dialogue form. Provide time for students to act out their new scripts for the rest of the group. Notice the variety of versions that emerge.

G-I-A-N-T Bingo

Make a copy of page 71 for each student. Have students copy the Fin vocabulary words in random order in the spaces provided. Then write each of the vocabulary words on an index card and place in a shoe box. One student, the caller, calls out (in order) each of the letters in the word GIANT followed by a vocabulary word to correspond to the letter (for example, G-Fin, I-Cucullin). When a vocabulary word appears under the correct letter, as indicated by the caller, students cover the space with a marker. The winner is the first player to cover the entire card and to call out "GIANT!"

Fin M'Coul

G	I	A	N	T

Vocabulary Words

Fin
M'Coul

giant
Irish

glens
Ireland
strong
glutton

woods
Irish
Oonagh
bully

brass
braid
Cucullin
stone

71

Harriet Tubman: They Call Me Moses

by Linda D. Meyer (Parenting Press, Inc. 1988)

Harriet Tubman tells her own story in this biography aimed at helping young children understand the pain of slavery and the pride of freedom. Tubman's life stands as a tribute to the strength of one woman who cared about herself and her people.

Exploring Themes of Slavery and Freedom

○ Help children to understand the evolution of slavery in America. Locate Africa and the United States on the map. Indicate how Africans were taken from their homes and families, and forced to travel by ship to America where they were put to work on plantations. Explain to children that many Americans (mostly those living in the South who needed laborers for plantations) approved of slavery.

○ In the book, Harriet says the time came when "I couldn't be another man's property anymore. I had to run. I had to own myself." Ask the class to tell in their own words what Harriet must have been feeling before and after she ran to freedom.

FOLLOW-UP ACTIVITIES

Freedom Chart

Create a chart designed to help children understand why Harriet Tubman worked so hard to free herself and others from slavery. Divide a poster-size piece of paper into four columns. Label the first column "Freedom" and have children use this column to list simple but important freedoms they enjoy. These may include the freedom to be part of a family: the freedom to make friends; the freedom to travel; the freedom to earn and spend money; the freedom to go to school; the freedom to read books; and the freedom to eat, sleep, and work when they (and their families) want. Label the second column "Importance" and have children tell why each freedom is important to them. Label the third column "Slavery" and use this space to write a list (corresponding to the first two columns) describing what happened when freedoms were taken from slaves (for example, "Slaves were often sold and separated from their families," "Slaves could not leave the plantation," etc.). In the last column, labeled "Feelings," have the children tell how they would feel if each freedom was taken away from them.

Freedom	Importance	Slavery	Feelings

A Classroom Family of Helpers

Reproduce copies of page 73. Then have children use markers, crayons, and glued on details (cut from fabric scraps, wallpaper samples, and construction paper) to make dolls that resemble themselves. Bind the pages together into a class collaborative. Make a cover and title page for your book. Have each child dictate or write a sentence about how they can help each other in their classroom family. Print sentence on the page facing the child's own self-portrait.

Harriet Tubman

Paper "Doll" outline

Laura Ingalls Wilder

by Gwenda Blair
(G. P. Putnam's Sons, 1981)

This is the story of a strong, independent little pioneer girl growing up more than a century ago on the American Frontier. Young readers will enjoy learning more about Laura's adventuresome life, which served as rich inspiration for her popular Little House *series of books.*

Exploring Themes of Moving and Hardships

○ Laura Ingalls Wilder moved many times in her life. Have the class skim the book and list all the places Laura called home. How were her homes the same and how were they different? Have the class relate their own experiences of moving or traveling. Ask: What are the positive and negative aspects of leaving a familiar place and moving on to a new one?

○ Have the class recall the many hardships Laura and her family endured in their life on the frontier. Ask: What may have helped them to stay brave and keep trying and moving on?

FOLLOW-UP ACTIVITIES

Leading the Blind

When Laura's sister Mary went blind, Laura had to be Mary's eyes. Have the children take turns leading classmates around the classroom blindfolded. Each leader should help the "blind" child "see" the room through description and touch. After every child has had a chance to be blindfolded, talk with the group about the experience. How would they feel and how would their lives change if the condition was permanent? If possible, provide the children with samples of Braille to touch and "read."

Little House Read Aloud

Regularly schedule a small amount of time each day for children to take turns reading favorite passages from some of the *Little House* series of books by Laura Ingalls Wilder.

Small Stories

Laura Ingalls Wilder got much pleasure from sharing the story of her life with others through her writing. Help children understand that the story of someone's life is really comprised of a series of smaller stories. Have each student record one small story from his or her life. Impress upon the children that their essays should be autobiographical—true stories about themselves. Encourage students to put as much detail as they can into their stories. Remind them that the best stories enable the reader to see and feel what the author saw and felt. Final versions of their stories may be transferred onto copies of page 75.

Laura Ingalls Wilder

Lion Dancer

by Kate Waters
(Scholastic Inc., 1990)

This is the true story of Ernie Wan, a Chinese boy looking forward to celebrating Chinese New Year. This year, Ernie will perform his first lion dance on the streets of New York City. Young readers will relish the rich color photos of Ernie and his family as they celebrate this special day together.

Exploring Themes of Anticipation and Pride

❍ Ask children to find the parts in the book where it shows how excited Ernie is about performing his lion dance. Have the children tell about special times they looked forward to. How were their feelings the same as or different from Ernie's?

❍ Ernie wanted the lion dance to bring honor to his family. He and his father were proud of his performance. Ask children to explain the difference between having a sense of pride and feeling that you're better than others. Ask: What's the best way to always feel proud of yourself?

FOLLOW-UP ACTIVITIES

Wok Cooking

Bring a wok to class and cook your favorite Chinese recipe with the group. Teach students how to eat their meal with chopsticks. For homework, have children write step-by-step directions for cooking in a wok and eating with chopsticks.

Chinese Horoscope Graph

Cover a bulletin board with plain paper. Draw a graph grid on the board (as indicated in the illustration). Draw the 12 Chinese horoscope symbols (as shown in the book) in the vertical spaces along the left-hand side of the board. Provide students with three index cards. Have children interview friends and family to find out the years they were born. Each card should record someone's name and year of birth. Students then attach cards to the board indicating each person's appropriate horoscope. Challenge the class to completely fill the graph with cards. Find out if children agree with the horoscope descriptions of their friends and family.

(rat)	Cindy Jones 1972	Kacy Cota 1972					
(ox)	Jerry Frank 1949	John Peters 1949	Kim Christy 1973	Tisha Moore 1973			
(tiger)	Nancy Ginn 1950	Anna Walls 1950					
(rabbit)	Michael Smith 1975	Oscar Edwards 1951	Sara Ward 1987	Terry Romo 1927			
(dragon)	Davina Gomez 1976	David Edwards 1976	Michaela Doherty 1988	Ben Moore 1988			
(snake)	Gabriel Gomez 1953	Mona Jones 1953					
(horse)	Peter Johns 1978						
(goat)	Richard Michaels 1955	Drew Andrews 1991	Kyle Andrews 1991	Veronica Ford 1967	Aaron Charles 1967		
(monkey)	Mike Patrick 1956						
(rooster)	Olivia Levy 1957						
(dog)	Adam Walls 1982	Steven Robles 1982	Cathy Cota 1958				
(pig)	Matthew Walls 1983						

Dragon Stick Puppets

Provide each student with two copies of the dragon on page 77. For each dragon puppet have children cut out two dragons, then decorate dragons using markers and paints. Then glue on glitter, feathers, and sequins. Fold a rectangle of oaktag in half lengthwise. Staple closed to create a dowel. Place oaktag "dowel" between the two dragons and glue them together. Allow to dry and staple lengths of crepe paper on dragon to create a tail. Have children parade their dragons to other classes to introduce a shared reading of *Lion Dancer.*

Lion Dancer

Spring Celebrations

Peter Spier's Rain

by Peter Spier
(Doubleday, 1982)

In this wordless picture book, we tag along as two children explore their neighborhood on a rainy day. The author skillfully helps the reader see an ordinary rainstorm as a lush, sensory experience.

Exploring Themes of Sensory Surprises and Changes

❍ In *Rain,* Peter Spier transforms the mood of the story through settings and weather. (The characters are first shown playing in a sunny outdoor scene. A rainstorm begins and the children continue to play outdoors. The storm then intensifies until the characters are forced to move indoors to a warmer, cozier setting. The next day's morning sunshine signifies a completion of the weather-dependent mood cycle.) Talk about effects the weather has on our moods. Does rainy weather always have to "go away" for us to feel happy? What other possible mood reactions could the children have to the weather changes in the story?

FOLLOW-UP ACTIVITIES

Splashy Pictures

Have the students discuss their own rainy day experiences. Then ask them to paint pictures depicting their experiences. Dip toothbrushes in blue paint (non-toxic or watercolor liquid paint solutions) and then, while holding the brush over each painting, run a craft stick or tongue depressor (away from you) over the bristles of the brush, causing the paint to "rain" on the painting. When paintings are dry, have the children share the paintings with the group.

Sunny Day Follow-Up

The *Rain* book concludes with the children looking out at the dawn of a new sunny day. Have students imagine how the characters spend the sunny day and then create a *Rain* sequel. Students can incorporate the same characters and the same settings in their sunny day illustrations. Collect and bind these into a wordless class collaborative entitled *Sun!*

Sensory Graph

In the book, two children explore their neighborhood on a rainy day. The children use their senses of sight, hearing, and touch to enjoy the day. Have your class take a second look at the book, noting which senses the characters were using in each picture. Distribute copies of page 81. Have each student use this page to make a bar graph noting the frequency of sight, sound, and tactile experiences as they appear in the book. (Your students will discover that some illustrations show the characters using more than one sense at a time.) Compare and discuss results.

Rain

Taste	Sight	Hearing	Smell	Touch

Henry and Mudge in Puddle Trouble

by Cynthia Rylant
(Bradbury Press, 1987)

Henry and his dog Mudge are featured in three separate springtime adventures. Henry and Mudge in Puddle Trouble *introduces readers to the wonderful world of "chapter books." And it provides a fresh springboard for some springtime learning fun.*

Exploring Themes of Naughtiness and Jealousy

❍ "Bad dog!" That's what Henry almost says to Mudge when he eats the Snow Glory flower. Have students imagine they are in Mudge's place. What would Mudge say if he could talk? Did he mean to be naughty? Did he mean to make Henry sad or angry?

❍ Ask: How do you know how Mudge feels about the kittens next door— and the new dog who tries to visit them? Transform Mudge's barks and snaps into words. Demonstrate the kind of voice he would use. Why do you think Mudge would speak this way? What would the new dog reply. In the story, Mudge makes the new dog go away. Create a new ending to the story.

> ## FOLLOW-UP ACTIVITIES

Pretend Puddle Play

Try the following ideas for acting out *Puddle Trouble:*

1. Have one student read the story aloud while other students act it out. Make labels printed with the characters' names (Henry, Mudge, and Dad). Have actors wear the labels while "on stage."

2. Divide the class into groups of three. Have the small groups work together to rewrite the story as a skit. Then have each group perform their skit for the class. How similar or different were the groups' interpretations of the story?

3. Have small groups work together to pantomime the stories in *Henry and Mudge in Puddle Trouble.* Show children how exaggerated movements can help to tell a story without words.

Kittens Symmetry

Provide students with copies of page 83. Have each student decorate the half of a kitten with stripes, spots, or both. Then have children exchange papers with a partner, and have the partner try to match the markings on the other side. When students have finished decorating their kittens, fold papers in half along the dotted lines, hold up to a window, and see if the markings line up. Variation: Have students paint one half of each kitten. While paint is still wet, fold paper closed, press, and carefully reopen. Observe transferred design. If desired, cut kittens out and mount on bulletin board as shown in illustration.

Now One Foot, Now the Other

by Tomie dePaola
(G. P. Putnam's Sons, 1981)

This is the story of a special relationship between a boy and his grandfather. As the boy grows, it is grandfather who teaches him how to walk. As the grandfather ages (and suffers a stroke), the boy returns the favor by helping his convalescing grandfather learn to walk all over again. Together they prove that the changes they experience are no barriers to the ageless love they feel for each other.

Exploring Themes of Caring and Change

❍ Bobby and Bob spend time together enjoying some favorite activities. List these on a chart pad. Lengthen the list by including those activities that students enjoy doing with their grandparents (or other favorite grown-ups). Have children sign and illustrate their contributions.

❍ Invite a mom to bring in a baby who is still learning to walk, or have the children bring in video tapes of themselves learning how to walk. Ask: Is it easy to learn how to walk? How long does it take to learn? Do babies ever think, "Walking is too hard. I'm giving up!"?

FOLLOW-UP ACTIVITIES

Photo Opportunities

Have children collect and take turns sharing photos of themselves and of older family members or friends. If possible, have the photos represent a variety of age spans (for example, pictures of the child could include those taken at the baby and toddler stages, while photos of the older person could include high school photos, wedding portraits, etc.). Ask the group to observe how the people in the photos changed and how they stayed the same. Offer each child colorful index cards on which to write captions for their pictures (including names of subject(s), date taken, place taken, occasion, etc.). Have each child arrange his or her photo collection in sequence according to time taken, and then attach photos and captions to a bulletin board entitled "Picture Us Growing and Changing."

Generations Tea

Invite grandparents or "honorary grandparents" to your class for an elegant tea party. Use markers, watercolor paints, or crayons to decorate copies of the invitation on page 85. Have each child draw his or her head popping out of the tea cup. Send invitations home along with a notice asking to borrow real tablecloths and cloth napkins for the occasion. The day before the tea, have children prepare finger foods such as small sandwiches, cookies, and bite-size muffins. Also, have each student bring two real tea cups and saucers (or mugs) and two teaspoons to school. You should provide tea bags, tea pots, sugar, milk, and lemon. The morning of the tea, push desks together banquet-style and cover with tablecloths. Review the list of hosting responsibilities with students (making introductions, serving food, showing guests around the class, etc.). When the guests have arrived and refreshments have been served, share a favorite book or song.

Come join me
and my class in
a cup of tea!
(Think we'll fit?)

Date ~~Dec~~ ~~July~~ Septemer

Time _____

Location _____

RSVP 206-1190

Hope you can drop in!

The Wednesday Surprise

by Eve Bunting
(Clarion Books, 1989)

Surprises are sprinkled throughout this story involving the love between a young girl and her grandmother. As the characters plan surprises for each other, the author plans one big surprise for the reader.

Exploring Themes of Loving Surprises and Late-Life Learning

○ At the start of *The Wednesday Surprise,* we know Anna and Grandma are planning a birthday surprise for Anna's father, but we don't know that the author is planning a surprise for us, too. Where does the author surprise us? (The author expects us to assume that Grandma already knows how to read.) Have children tell about times they planned (rather than purchased) loving surprises for grandparents or other grown-ups.

○ Grandma tells Sam, "It's much smarter if you learn to read when you're young. The chance may pass along with the years." What message was Grandma trying to pass on to Sam? Are some things easier to learn when we're young? Why? Have children ask grown-ups what things they wish they had learned when they were young and what new things they are learning now? Plan time for children to report findings to the group.

FOLLOW-UP ACTIVITIES

New View Books

Because *The Wednesday Surprise* is written from Anna's point of view, we get a peek inside her mind and heart. Have children rewrite the story from an older character's viewpoint (Grandma's, Dad's, or Mom's). Ask: How does this character feel as the story unfolds? Have children illustrate their stories. Staple the papers together and cover stapled edge with fabric tape.

Buddy Bookmarks

Reproduce childrens' school photos (or other full-face photos of students) on a copy machine. Trim around heads and glue them onto 8-by-4-inch rectangles of oaktag. Have students use fine-line markers to draw bodies on the heads and then color heads and bodies with colored pencils. Cover paper people bookmarks with clear adhesive paper, or laminate for durability. Have students present bookmarks to adults who enjoy reading, or to senior reading buddies.

Shared Book Report

Provide children with copies of "Shared Book Report" on page 87. Then, after reading a favorite book with an older family member or friend, have them record their reactions to the book together. Display these reports on a bulletin board entitled: "Favorite Books for the Young and the Young at Heart." If possible, complete the board with snapshots of children and their senior reading partners.

The Wednesday Surprise

Do this report with your reading buddy. Be sure to sign your names after each part you write!

Shared Book Report

by _____ and _____

Book Title _____

Book Author _____

Tell why you did or did not like the book.

_____   _____
_____   _____
_____   _____
_____   _____
_____   _____

If you could be a character in the story, who would you be and why?

_____   _____
_____   _____
_____   _____
_____   _____
_____   _____

On the back of this paper, draw your favorite scene from the book.

Bikes

by Anne Rockwell
(E. P. Dutton, 1987)

Bikes and more bikes are featured in this easy-to-read bike primer. Children will love comparing and contrasting all the varieties of bikes illustrated here. And they'll be delighted to discover that bikes are fun for everyone from babies to grown-ups!

Exploring Themes of Bike Types

❍ Have children count the number of bike types in the book. How many wheels are pictured on each bike? How many wheels are pictured in the book? How many wheels are pictured on motorized bikes? Subtract this figure from the total number of wheels. Ask children to guess what this difference represents (the number of wheels on non-motorized bikes).

FOLLOW-UP ACTIVITIES

Vehicle Fair

Invite students to bring their vehicles (skateboards, bikes, skates, scooters, etc.) to school. Have them also bring in decorative ribbons and bows from home. Use these to decorate the vehicles. Parade vehicles in a protected area (a playground or park). Have children take turns demonstrating the proper way to use their vehicles.

Vehicle Collages

Have children clip pictures of vehicles from magazines and catalogs. Trim photos. Create collages by gluing pictures onto construction paper. Begin by gluing large pictures in the center of the paper and then overlap with smaller pictures. Brush completed collages with a wash of white glue and water.

Magnetic Bicycle Story Boards

Give each child a copy of page 89. Paste them on construction paper trimmed to fit. Have children use markers and crayons to decorate roads with buildings, trees, road signs, people, and more. Cut vehicles apart, fold along dotted lines, and attach a paper clip to the base of each. Manipulate vehicle along road by moving a magnet beneath the paper. Have children describe the sites their vehicles pass en route. Challenge them to create additional vehicles to move along the road. (Hint: Copies of page 89 may be placed together to make a larger map for use as a floor mat for classroom toy vehicles.)

Bikes

Story Board Map

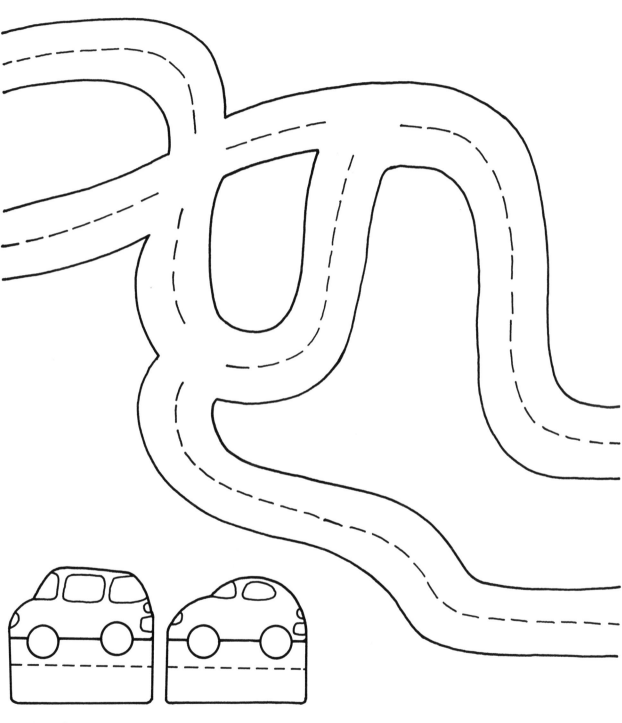

Vehicles

The Bicycle Man

by Allen Say
(Parnassus Press Book, 1982)

The setting is sports day at an elementary school in post World War II Japan. The story is told from the perspective of a Japanese child who meets two American soldiers—one African American, one Caucasian—for the first time. The children are frightened of the Americans, but when one soldier demonstrates daring tricks on a bicycle, the soldiers are regarded as friends.

Exploring Themes of Prejudice and Admiration

❍ Help the children understand the significance of having two American soldiers visit a Japanese school during the post-World War II occupation. Have the class discuss how the war may or may not have affected the Japanese students' feelings about Americans.

❍ Ask: How are the students' and soldiers' feelings towards one another affected by the sports-day visit? It's clear that the Japanese students admire the soldier for his performance on the bike. Challenge the children to explore other (more subtle) ways the children may have admired the soldiers (for their friendliness, their ability to have fun, etc.). How may the soldiers have admired the students (for their ability to give the soldiers a chance to play, their ability to offer cheerful support to the demonstration, etc.)?

FOLLOW-UP ACTIVITIES

A Peek at Prejudice

Have the class discuss what they believe is meant by the word *prejudice* then look it up in the dictionary. Have the children explain how *The Bicycle Man* is a story showing how prejudice can cloud good judgement. Give each student three pieces of paper. Label the first page, "People," the second page "Places," and the last page "Things." Under each category, have children tell about people, places, and things that they have prejudged, the criteria on which the judgment was made, and why their prejudices were proven wrong. Invite children to share their completed lists with the group. Explain that it is experience that helps us to make better judgments.

Bicycle Shape Books

Give each student several copies of page 91. Have students cut out bicycles (along heavy line) and glue* onto sheets of white or manila paper. Then have students illustrate themselves doing daring tricks on the bicycle. (Illustrations should show all the steps of the trick.) Encourage students to draw ground lines and add colorful background details. Have students write about what is happening in each picture and staple the pictures together in the form of a book. Schedule time for would-be trick riders to share their books. (This is a good time to review bicycle safety rules!)

　*Because students may want to rotate the position of the bicycle during the trick, have them glue the bicycles down permanently only *after* they have decided on their story line.

The Bicycle Man

Bicycle Safety Tips

1. Keep away from busy streets.

2. Make sure your bicycle works well. Fix loose or broken parts.

3. Keep both hands on the handlebars.

4. Walk your bicycle across streets.

5. At corners, stop, look, and listen for other people and cars.

6. Use hand signals.

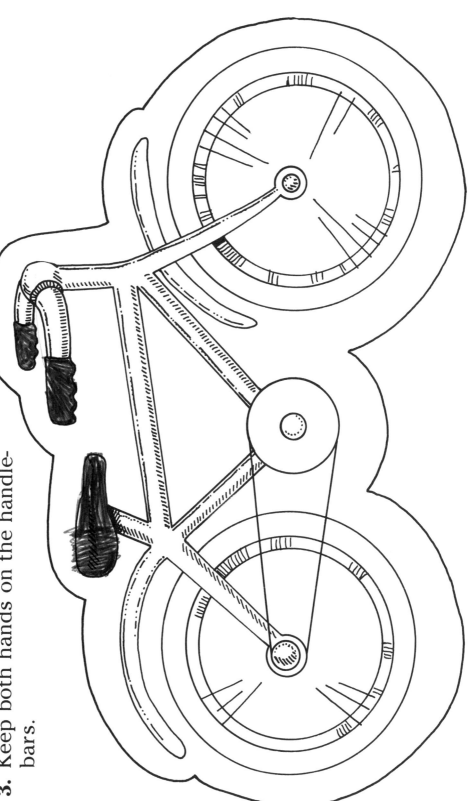

Rain Forest

by Helen Cowcher
(Farrar, Straus and Giroux, 1988)

The exotic creatures of the rain forest live in harmony. Then a terrible monster threatens this peaceful kingdom. At the book's conclusion, the reader is left wondering whether the rain forest and its inhabitants will ever survive the damage that's been dealt.

Exploring Themes of Danger and Destruction

○ Discuss how it feels to be in danger. Have students relate stories about times they've had brushes with danger. List these on a chart pad or on the chalkboard. How were the potentially dangerous situations alike?

○ Ask the children to comment on the destruction of the rain forest as portrayed in the book. Were the machines (or the machine operators) responsible for the cutting and the spoiling? Why did the man run his machine through the rain forest? Make a list of possible reasons for the destruction. Do any of the reasons justify the destruction?

> ## FOLLOW-UP ACTIVITIES

"Save the Rain Forest" Exhibit

Raise your class's rain forest consciousness by planning a rain forest exhibit including the following ideas. Then, open your exhibit to the rest of the school and make everyone aware of the plight of the rain forest.

1. **Rain-Forest Research**

   Have children research the following rain-forest facts: where it is; why it's important; what animals inhabit the rain forest; what plants grow in the rain forest; what threatens the rain forest. Have children hang these lists around the room. Share rain forest videos with the class. Later, you can play them for visitors.

2. **Rain-Forest Stuffed-Animal Sculptures**

   After students discover which animals live in the rain forest, place transparencies of these animals on an overhead projector and project images onto sheets of butcher paper. Trace animals and cut two of each. Staple the two pieces together and cover the edges with masking tape, leaving an opening. Have children paint animals. When dry, stuff with newspaper and staple shut. Display around the room.

3. **Rain-Forest Reading**

   Have students take turns reading *Rain Forest* for visitors. Also, plan times for students to share what they know about the animals they researched.

4. **Rain-Forest Mix Recipe**

   Offer visitors a snack of rain-forest products. Have children find out what edible goodies are grown in the rain forest (Brazil nuts, cashews, bananas, figs, etc.). Combine these products in a large bowl (making sure the fruits are dried). Next to the bowl, place a large sign reading, "Taste the Gifts of the Rain Forest."

5. **Rain-Forest Exhibit Invitations**

   Print copies of the invitation on page 93 (preferably on recycled paper). Have students use vibrant colors to complete and decorate the invitations. Have students clip along the dotted lines to create "doors" in the foliage. Bend doors forward and glue the invitation to construction paper. Have children write information regarding exhibit date, time, etc. under the leaves.

Rain Forest

Exhibit Invitations

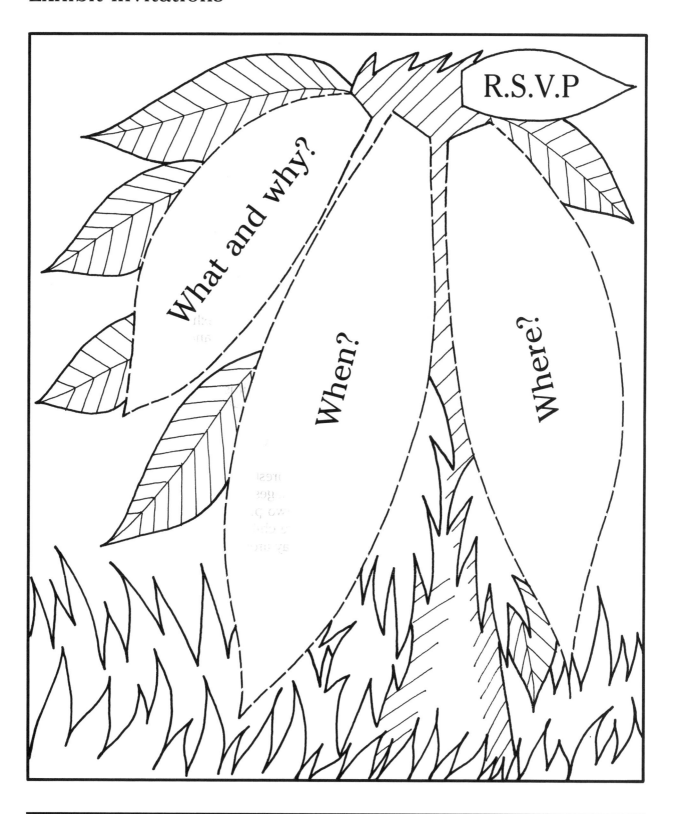

The Wump World

by Bill Peet
(Houghton Mifflin Co., 1970)

Wump World is a peaceable place and the Wumps have no enemies. Then, iron and steel monsters from the planet Pollutus shatter the security of the Wump's gentle kingdom. The thinly veiled irony here shows that while we all want to live in a safe, clean, and happy world, we're also responsible for behaving like the careless Pollutians. The book ends with a note of cautious optimism.

Exploring Themes of Selfishness and Responsibility

○ Have children list the environmentally negative practices of the Pollutians. How did each practice hurt Wump World? Have children list some environmentally negative practices in our world. How do our practices hurt the earth and the atmosphere? (Children may need to research the negative effects of practices such as littering.)

○ When the effects of the Pollutians' bad practices made Wump World a terrible place to live, the Pollutians left for greener pastures. What other choices did the Pollutians have? Why would it be a good or bad idea for us to leave Earth when it becomes too polluted.

FOLLOW-UP ACTIVITIES

Photo Essay: Do's and Don'ts for Earth

Take the class on a neighborhood walk. Have children take turns photographing positive and negative environmental practices. (If possible use an instant camera for immediate photo-feedback.) Back in the classroom, divide a bulletin board into two sections. One section should be labeled "Do Help the Earth," and the other section labeled, "Don't Hurt the Earth." Have students sort and display the photographs under the appropriate heading. Ask students to print explanatory captions beneath each picture.

Grass for the Wumps

Have each child bring a large sponge to school. Rinse each sponge under water and place in a dish. Sprinkle the sponge with grass seed and place in a sunny spot. (Be sure the location does not become too hot, or grass will burn.) Keep the sponge moist by spraying daily with a water mist. After grass has sprouted, have children draw Wumps on paper (or make them out of brown pom-poms and tiny eyes available in craft stores). Attach Wumps to toothpicks and stick them into the sponge. These should remind children to treat their world as gently as the Wumps treated Wump World.

Ecology Dilemma Cards

Make a copy of page 95. Separate the cards and place them in a pocket on the "Do's and Don'ts" bulletin board (or in a shoe box). Have students take turns selecting a card. After reading the dilemma on the card, have the group discuss the problem and brainstorm possible solutions. Encourage a variety of solutions to the dilemma. (Note: If a student suggests a grandiose solution to a problem, for example, "I want to clean all the rivers in the world," accept and acknowledge the student's enthusiasm while refocusing the students on efforts they can manage themselves. Cards may also be used as springboards to writing essays on how to save the environment.

Ecology Dilemma Cards

You want to cut down on your use of paper. How can you begin to conserve?

You see a grown-up you know throw garbage on the ground. What should you do?

You want your family to save water, but they think it's too much trouble. What should you do?

Someone you love is polluting the air by smoking. Should you tell them to stop?

You see your friend throw a candy wrapper on the ground. Should you tell your friend not to litter? Why?

You want to help keep the air clean, but your friends say air pollution isn't your problem. What should you do?

Laura Charlotte

by Kathryn O. Galbraith
(Philomel Books, 1990)

A mother, a daughter, and a beloved stuffed elephant named Charlotte remind us that simple stories of thoughtfulness and generosity are the glue that can hold generations of a family together.

Exploring Themes of Family History and Treasured Keepsakes

○ *Laura Charlotte* shows how stories handed down from generation to generation can serve to connect family members. Have children share stories they've heard from the grown-ups in their family. What stories from their own childhood will they pass on to their children?

○ *Laura Charlotte* also shows how memorabilia can connect generations. Have children show-and-tell (or just tell about) special objects that have been handed down in their families, relaying as much information as possible about the age, origin, and significance of the object. Label and display the objects (or drawings of the objects) for all to enjoy.

FOLLOW-UP ACTIVITIES

Antique Toy Share

Invite parents to bring their old toys to class. Have parents share stories about their playthings. Have students prepare questions (What games did they play with their toys? Did they ever play make-believe? Who did they play with? How are the parents' toys the same or different from toys of today?)

Elephant Stitchery

Using pinking scissors and the outline of the elephant on page 97 for a pattern, cut elephants from scraps of fabric. Give each child a piece of burlap (approximately 10 by 12 inches). Show students how to stitch elephants onto burlap as illustrated. Wrap hanger hook with masking tape. Fold top edge of burlap over wire hanger as shown. Stitch in place. Hang to display.

— Burlap

— Glue on felt eyes and tusks.

— "In and out" running stitch

Elephant Memory Mobiles

Have each student bring in small photos of at least six family members (extended family included), or provide small pieces of paper on which students can draw family members' faces. Trace the elephant pattern on pages 97 onto light gray oaktag. Cut apart body parts as shown. Punch a hole in the top of each piece. On the reverse side of each piece, glue one family member's photo or portrait. Arrange the elephant pieces on table. Knot a length of yarn to each piece and measure evenly to reach a hanger. Tie yarn to hanger whose hook has been wrapped in masking tape. Hang elephant against a wall. Turn pieces to reveal elephant or photos.

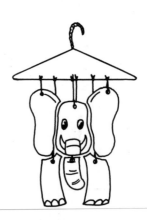

Laura Charlotte

Elephant Pattern

My Father Doesn't Know About the Woods and Me

by Dennis Haseley
(Antheneum Books, 1988)

In this lovely ethereal story, a woodland walk helps a son discover a natural link to his father. Lush, textured paintings of woods and wildlife complement the secretive, sensuous text.

Exploring Themes of Secrets and Similarities

❍ The boy in the book believes he keeps a secret from his father. Ask the group to share their feelings about keeping secrets. When are secrets okay? Is it ever wrong to keep secrets?

❍ Ask students to explain how the boy in the book is like his father. Then encourage them to describe how their feelings and experiences are like those of their own parents or other adults they know. How are they different?

FOLLOW-UP ACTIVITIES

School Family-Tree Leaf Prints

Cover a wall with light blue paper. Place a tree stencil on an overhead projector and aim the image at the paper. Paint the tree. Collect leaves from outdoors. Paint the underneath side of each leaf with tempera paints. Create leaf prints by pressing paint-covered leaves onto the tree. Invite children to print the names of schoolmates and school personnel on the leaves. Finish display with the heading "Our School Family Tree."

Woodland Images

As a relaxation exercise, have students close their eyes and lie down (or put their heads on their desks). Then, take the group on an imaginary walk in the woods. In a quiet voice, describe how the setting looks, feels, sounds, and smells. Describe the foliage, the sky, the temperature, and the wildlife. Describe a babbling brook, a sunny, warm clearing, and a cool, mossy spot. Then, lead the group back to the starting point of the exercise and have them slowly open their eyes. Repeat the exercise, this time having a student guide the class to a favorite place.

Woodland Transformations

Have students imagine they have been transformed into a woodland creature of their choice. Have them draw themselves (and any other woodland details they wish) on the woodland story frame on page 99. They can cover the whole page, but have them draw very lightly with colored pencils. Then have students write about a typical day. What do they eat? What do they learn? Do they have to work? Are their any dangers? Students may write polished essays directly over their artwork (or the artwork may serve as a cover for the essay).

My Father Doesn't Know About the Woods and Me

Woodland Story Frame

Pet Show

by Ezra Jack Keats
(Macmillan, 1972)

Everyone is talking about the pet show. Archie plans to enter his cat in the contest, but his cat disappears the morning of the show. To join in the pet-show fun, Archie quickly relies on his ingenuity and creativity. And, in the end, we see how Archie's generous nature helps him win more than just a pet-show ribbon.

Exploring Themes of Pet Care and Winning

❍ Poll your class to discover the kinds and number of pets they own. (Children who do not own pets can talk about the kind of animals they would most like to care for.) Invite children to have their pets visit your classroom. Specify time parameters for the visits and request that visiting pets be accompanied by a parent or other adult. Develop a list of questions for the pet owners. How did they come to own their pets? What routines do they follow to keep pets happy and healthy.

❍ In the book, the judges think Archie's cat belongs to a woman, and they award her a ribbon for "the cat with the longest whiskers." Ask students if they agree or disagree with Archie's decision to let the woman keep the ribbon. Have them tell in their own words how Archie must have felt at that moment. Direct children's attention to the picture of Archie watching the woman win the ribbon. (Point out that the ribbon is a bright spot in an otherwise dark illustration.) Does the illustration give us any hints about what Archie and the woman are feeling and thinking?

Shadow-Puppet Pet Show

Have you own pet show using shadow puppets! Copy and cut out shapes on page 103. Place shapes on an overhead projector. Enlarge and project images onto heavy craft paper taped to the wall. Trace the images, cut them out, and tape them to craft sticks or dowels to make puppets. Cut a large rectangle in the bottom of a large cardboard box and cover the opening with a piece of thin white craft paper. Tape this paper "screen" securely in place. Place the puppet theatre on a table. Provide backlighting (a lamp, flashlight, etc.) to illuminate puppets from behind. Invite puppeteers to retell *Pet Show!*, or have them create their own pet stories.

Paper-Bag Pets

Provide children with paper bags and decorative art materials (crayons, markers, paints, yarn, googlie eyes, pipe cleaners, sticky dots, fabric scraps and trims, etc.) Have children decorate bags to make paper-bag pet puppets, or stuff bags with crumpled newspaper, staple shut, and decorate. (Weight stuffed bags with oaktag "feet" or bases to allow animals to stand freely.) If desired, enter pets in a pet show and decide together on an award for each pet (most lovable, most original, quietest pet, etc.). Award each pet a personalized copy of the certificate on page 101.

Date: _Sally Best_

Pet's name: _Wrinkels_

Awarded for: _Best and funniest and coolest face_

Awarded by: _____

P.E.T. AWARD

That Dog!

by Nanette Newman
(Thomas Y. Crowell, 1983)

Ben and his dog Barnum are best friends—they do everything together. Then one day Barnum dies, leaving Ben alone and lonely. How Ben survives the loss of his best friend (and how he moves on to make another canine friend) will remind readers of the important places pets hold in peoples' lives and hearts.

Exploring Themes of Friendship and Loss

❍ Have the children talk about their favorite animals. How many different types of pets make different types of friends? Have children cite parts of the book showing how Ben feels about Barnum? How do the other characters in the book feel about Barnum?

❍ When Barnum dies, Ben "felt as if his heart had been broken." He also cried, was late for school, and didn't feel like playing soccer. Have children talk about times they may have felt sad. What helped them to feel better?

FOLLOW-UP ACTIVITIES

Coping with Loss

When Barnum dies, Ben must cope with a *loss*. Talk with the children to see how much they understand about the concept of loss. Develop a list of losses the children have experienced. Encourage students to share examples of both large and small losses. Examine the list together and talk about a variety of possible reactions and feelings which could result from each loss. Help the class understand that people may act differently when experiencing a loss, but that they often share the same feelings inside.

Pet Biographies

Have children write biographies of pets they own or pets they know. Biographies should tell how the animal came to live with its owner. They should also include the animal's birthplace (date and location), history (including any mishaps or visits to the vet), and personality (favorite foods, likes, dislikes, friends, habits, etc.).

Pet-Care Books (Shape Books)

Have each student select a favorite pet and research how to care for the pet. Begin by having children list what they know about pet care. (Show children how to use resources to verify any information listed.) For additional pet-care information, encourage children to visit the library. Also, ask local veterinarians for pet-care pamphlets. After the children have completed their research, have them divide the information into categories (feeding, grooming, exercise, vitamins, inoculations, etc.), which may serve as chapter headings for their books. When all the information has been gathered, have children write and illustrate their pet-care research in shape books. (Use an overhead projector to enlarge the patterns on page 103 to make animal shape books or create your own shapes.)

That Dog!

Animal Shape Books Patterns

We Are Best Friends

by Aliki
(Greenwillow Books, 1982)

Robert and Peter are best friends. They can't imagine being apart, but then Peter announces that he is moving away. Young readers will enjoy learning how the boys remain friends by slowly opening their hearts to new playmates.

Exploring Themes of Loneliness and New Kids

❍ After Peter moves away, Robert feels lonely even when other children are near. Ask the children to tell how it is possible to be lonely in a crowd. How would they feel if they were in Robert's shoes? What advice would they give to Robert?

❍ Ask children to describe how Robert feels when he first meets the new boy, Will. Show how and why Robert's feelings change as the story continues. Have children talk about times their feelings changed with time.

FOLLOW-UP ACTIVITIES

Waving Goodbye in Style

Cover a wall with craft paper, or for a more permanent display, get permission to print directly on a wall. Place paper towels on a stack of newspapers to create a giant stamp pad. Pour a small amount of pre-mixed paint onto the paper towels. Have children press their hands in the paint and make handprints on the wall. When dry, use markers to label handprints with students' names. To complete the display, add the heading: "Wave Goodbye to School, Wave Hello to Summer!"

Friendship Time Tubes

Have children illustrate times they have spent with best friends and then write or dictate descriptions beneath the illustrations. Be sure to date the illustrations. Decorate empty paper-towel tubes with paint and markers. Stack illustrations together, roll them, and place them inside the tube. Tuck the tube away for a lonely day (when some friendly memories will bring cheer).

Stay-In-Touch Fold-Over Notes

Provide children with copies of page 105. Practice preparing and sending notes. Have each student select a classmate's name. Use the notepaper to write a message or draw an illustration for this classmate. Help students properly complete addresses and return addresses. Show children how notes may be folded for mailing. Tape notes shut. Collect the notes and place them in a shoe box or cardboard mailbox. During the last month of school, choose one note a day to deliver to a student. Encourage children to use additional notes for summer correspondence with friends and family. (Remind the class that real mail requires real postage!)

We Are Best Friends

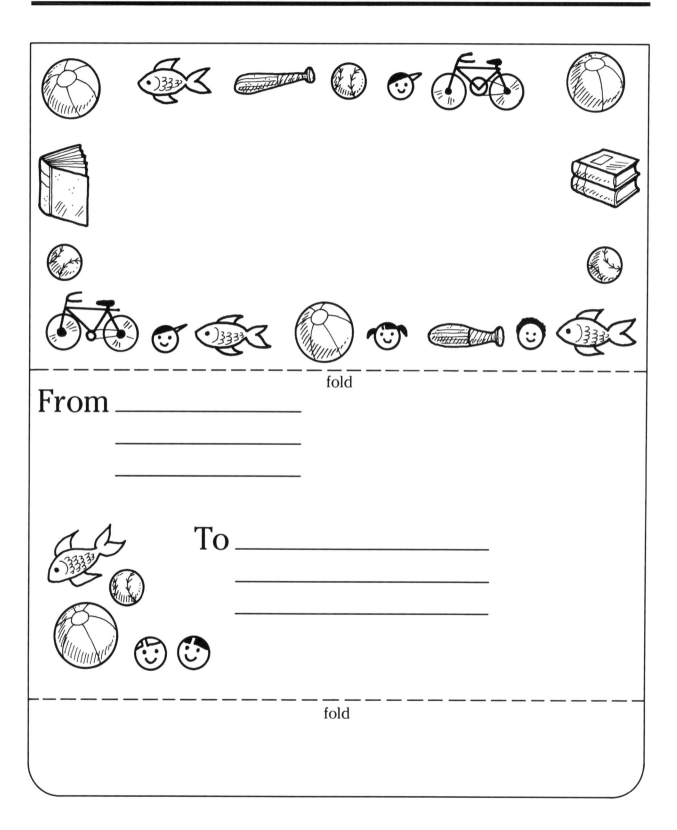

From _____

_____

_____

To _____

_____

_____

fold

fold

Ira Says Goodbye

by Bernard Waber
(Houghton Mifflin Co.)

Ira and Reggie are inseparable best friends. Nothing can come between them—nothing, that is, until Reggie learns he must move away. The friends find it difficult to deal honestly with their feelings. When Reggie and Ira finally face their sadness, they learn that saying goodbye to each other doesn't mean saying goodbye to their friendship.

Exploring Themes of Facing Feelings and Cheering Up

❍ Have students explain how Ira and Reggie are good examples of when people "lie to themselves." Why did Reggie say he was happy to be moving? Why did Ira say he couldn't wait for Reggie to move? When did the boys' true feelings come out? How did the boys feel once they admitted their honest feelings?

❍ Ask: How did Ira and Reggie say goodbye? How did Ira's family try to make him feel better? What else could they have done? Guess how Reggie's family helped him feel better. When you are sad, does it feel good if someone tells you to cheer-up? Why or why not?

Friendship Turtle Bracelet

Give each student a circle of corrugated cardboard (2 inches in diameter), two pieces of craft yarn (8 inches each), pre-mixed paint, fine-line markers, a pipe cleaner (cut to 6 inches), scissors, and cloth tape. Have children paint one side of the circle to resemble a turtle's back. When dry, add details with markers. Push pipe cleaner through the cardboard corrugation to create turtle tail and head. Curl head and tail toward turtle body. Turn turtle over. Place yarn across underside of turtle at spots where legs would be. Tape securely in place. Tie turtle to wrist with yarn legs.

Goodbye Cupcakes

Prepare cupcakes according to your favorite recipe, or follow directions on prepared mix package (check health-food store for best mix). Smooth vanilla frosting on cupcakes. Using a pastry bag, print one letter of a goodbye message (e.g. G-O-O-D B-Y-E F-O-R T-H-E S-U-M-M-E-R or G-O-O-D L-U-C-K I-N Y-O-U-R N-E-W S-C-H-O-O-L) on each cupcake with decorative icing. Extra cupcakes may be decorated with exclamation points.

Autograph Books

Reproduce copies of page 107. Cut pages in half as indicated and make holes with hole puncher. Bind together with yarn or inexpensive plastic shower-curtain rings. (You may want to reinforce holes with loose-leaf hole reinforcers). Tell children to use these pages to write goodbye message to each other. Remind students to date their entries.

Ira Says Goodbye

Pages for Autograph Books

Fall Celebrations

THE SEASON OF FALL

Ox-Cart Man by Donald Hall (Viking Press, 1979)

Henry and Mudge Under the Yellow Moon by Cynthia Rylant (Bradbury Press, 1987)

BACK TO SCHOOL

Will I Have a Friend? by Miriam Cohen (Macmillian, 1986)

Arthur's Teacher Trouble by Marc Brown (Joy Street Books, 1986)

DAY OF PEACE

Faithful Elephants: A True Story by Yukio Tsuchiya (Houghton Mifflin, 1988)

Peace Porridge No 1: Kids as Peacemakers by Teddy Milne (Pittenbruach Press, 1987)

NATIVE AMERICAN DAY

Good Hunting, Blue Sky by Peggy Parish (Harper, 1988)

Knots on a Counting Rope by Bill Martin (Henry Holt and Co., 1987)

DISCOVERERS' DAY

Christopher Columbus by Jan Gleiter and Kathleen Thompson (Raintree Publications, 1986)

STATUE OF LIBERTY ANNIVERSARY

Miss Liberty: First Lady of the World by June Behrens (Children's Press, 1986)

HALLOWEEN

George's Halloween by Robert Bright (Doubleday, 1958)

Arthur's Halloween by Marc Brown (Joy Street Books, 1982)

THANKSGIVING

Little Bear's Thanksgiving by Janice (Lothrop,Lee and Shepard, 1967)

Arthur's Thanksgiving by Marc Brown (Joy Street Books, 1983)

JOHNNY APPLESEED'S BIRTHDAY

The Seasons of Arnold's Apple Tree by Gail Gibbons (Harcourt Brace Jovanovich, 1988)

Johnny Appleseed and Other Poems by Vachel Lindsay (Buccaneer Books, 1981)

Winter Celebrations

THE SEASON OF WINTER

The Snowy Day by Ezra Jack Keats (Penguin, 1976)

The Black Snowman by Phil Mendez (Scholastic Inc., 1989)

CHRISTMAS

The Polar Express by Chris Van Allsburg (Houghton Mifflin, 1985)

Arthur's Christmas by Marc Brown (Joy Street Books, 1985)

CHANUKAH

The Chanukka Guest by Eric A. Kimmel (Holiday House, 1988)

We Celebrate Hanukkah by Bobbie Kalman (Crabtree Publishing Co.,
  1986)

MARTIN LUTHER KING DAY

Martin Luther King, Jr. Free at Last by David Adler (Holiday, 1986)

My First Martin Luther King Book by Dee Lillegard (Children's Press,
  1987)

VALENTINE'S DAY

"Bee My Valentine!" by Miriam Cohen (Greenwillow, 1978)

Don't Be My Valentine by Joan M. Lexau (Harper Collins, 1985)

PRESIDENTS' DAY

George Washington's Breakfast by Jean Fritz (Putnam, 1984)

Lincoln's Birthday by Clyde Bulla (Crowell, 1986)

ST. PATRICK'S DAY

Little Bear Marches in the St. Patrick's Day Parade (Lothrop, Lee and
  Shepard, 1967)

Tim O'Toole and the Little People by Gerald McDermott (Viking, 1990)

WOMEN'S NATIONAL HISTORY WEEK

Elizabeth Cady Stanton by Carol Hilgartner Schlank and Barbara Metzger
  (Gryphon House, 1991)

CHINESE NEW YEAR

Chinese New Year by Hou-Tien Cheng (Henry Holt and Co., 1976)

Spring Celebrations

THE SEASON OF SPRING

Over in the Meadow by Olive A. Wadsworth (Scholastic Inc., 1988)

Make Way for Ducklings by Robert McCloskey (Viking, 1941)

OLDER AMERICANS MONTH

Sea Swan by Kathryn Lasky (Macmillan, 1988)

My Grandma Has Black Hair by Mary Hoffman and Joanna Burroughs (Dial, 1988)

BIKE SAFETY WEEK

Angelina's Birthday Surprise by Katharine Holabird (Potter, 1989)

The Bike Lesson by Stan and Jan Bernstain (Beginner Books [Random House], 1964)

EARTH DAY

The Lorax by Dr. Seuss (Random House, 1971)

Just a Dream by Chris Van Allsburg (Houghton Mifflin, 1990)

NATIONAL FAMILY WEEK

Song and Dance Man by Karen Ackerman (Knopf, 1988)

Kevin's Grandma by Barbara Williams (Dutton, 1975)

BE KIND TO ANIMALS WEEK/NATIONAL PET WEEK

Be Kind to Animals by James Duffy (Western Publishers, 1988)

Scruffy by Peggy Parish (Harper Collins, 1988)

LEAVETAKINGS (COMMENCEMENTS, GOOD-BYES, ETC.)

See You in Second Grade by Miriam Cohen (Greenwillow, 1989)

List of Publishers

Addison-Wesley Publishing Co., Inc.
1 Jacob Way
Reading, MA 01867

Anthenum
866 Third Ave.
New York, NY 10022

Bradbury Press
866 Third Ave.
New York, NY 10022

Carolrhoda Books, Inc.
241 First Ave. N.
Minneapolis, MN 55401

Children's Press
1224 West Van Buren St.
Chicago, IL 60607

Clarion Books
215 Park Ave. S.
New York, NY 10003

E. P. Dutton
2 Park Ave.
New York, NY 10016

Farrar, Straus and Giroux
19 Union Square W.
New York NY 10003

GP Putnam's Sons
51 Madison Ave.
New York, NY 10010

Greenwillow Books
105 Madison Ave.
New York, NY 10016

Henry Holt and Co.
521 Fifth Ave.
New York, NY 10175

Houghton Mifflin Co.—Boston
2 Park St.
Boston, MA 02106

Kar-Ben Copies, Inc.
6800 Tildenwood Ln.
Rockville, MD 20852

Lothrop, Lee and Shepard Books
105 Madison Ave.
New York, NY 10016

Orchard Books
387 Park Ave.
New York, NY 10016

Parenting Press
7744 31st Ave. N.E.
Seattle, WA 98115

Parnassus Press Books
(Imprint of Houghton Mifflin Co.—Boston)
2 Park St.
Boston, MA 02106

Philomel Books
200 Madison Ave.
New York, NY 10016

Raintree Publishers, Inc.
310 W. Wisconsin Ave.
Milwaukee, WI 53203

Scholastic Inc.
730 Broadway
New York, NY 10003

Thomas Y. Crowell, Jr. Books
10 E. 53rd St.
New York, NY 10022

William Morrow and Co.
105 Madison Ave.
New York, NY 10016